AUSTRALIA'S UNIVERSITIES

Can They Reform?

Salvatore Babones

Contents

List of tables

List of figures

University abbreviations

ACU	Australian Catholic University
Adelaide	University of Adelaide
ANU	Australian National University
Batchelor	Batchelor Institute of Indigenous Tertiary Education
Canberra	University of Canberra
CDU	Charles Darwin University
CQU	Central Queensland University
CSU	Charles Sturt University
Curtin	Curtin University
Deakin	Deakin University
ECU	Edith Cowan University
Federation	Federation University Australia
Flinders	Flinders University
Griffith	Griffith University
JCU	James Cook University
La Trobe	La Trobe University
Macquarie	Macquarie University
Melbourne	University of Melbourne
Monash	Monash University
Murdoch	Murdoch University
Newcastle	University of Newcastle
Notre Dame	University of Notre Dame Australia
Queensland	University of Queensland
QUT	Queensland University of Technology
RMIT	Royal Melbourne Institute of Technology
SCU	Southern Cross University
Swinburne	Swinburne University of Technology

Sydney	University of Sydney
Tasmania	University of Tasmania
UNE	University of New England
UNISA	University of South Australia
UNSW	University of New South Wales
USC	University of the Sunshine Coast
USQ	University of Southern Queensland
UTS	University of Technology Sydney
UWA	University of Western Australia
Victoria	Victoria University
Wollongong	University of Wollongong
WSU	Western Sydney University

Other abbreviations

AACSB	Association to Advance Collegiate Schools of Business
ACRI	Australia-China Relations Institute
AFRA	Australia's Foreign Relations Act
AQF	Australian Qualifications Framework
ARC	Australian Research Council
ARWU	Academic Ranking of World Universities
ASPI	Australian Strategic Policy Institute
ATAR	Australian Tertiary Admission Rank
AVCC	Australian Vice-Chancellors' Committee (predecessor to Universities Australia)
CRICOS	Commonwealth Register of Institutions and Courses for Overseas Students
CSIRO	Commonwealth Scientific and Industrial Research Organisation
DESE	Department of Education, Skills and Employment
EFTSL	Equivalent full-time student load
FTE	Full-time equivalent
Go8	Group of Eight
GOS	Graduate Outcomes Survey
GOS-L	Graduate Outcomes Survey - Longitudinal
HCR	Highly Cited Researcher (Clarivate)
HESA	Higher Education Support Act
MOOC	Massive Open Online Course
NTEU	National Tertiary Education Union
OECD	Organisation for Economic Co-operation and Development
QILT	Quality Indicators for Learning and Teaching

QS	Quacquarelli Symonds
RSP	Research Support Program
RTP	Research Training Program
SCI	Science Citation Index
SES	Student Experience Survey
SSCI	Social Science Citation Index
STEM	Science, technology, engineering, and mathematics
TEQSA	Tertiary Education Quality and Standards Agency
THE	Times Higher Education

CHAPTER 1

Introduction: What are Australia's universities?

Australia's universities are in crisis. At a time when it has become *de rigueur* to describe everything as being 'in crisis', Australia's universities really are. They are suffering a pandemic-induced financial crisis brought on by travel restrictions that have prevented international students from entering the country. At the same time, most universities have suffered little-publicised—but much larger—declines in investment income. The coronavirus also forced an emergency shift to online education for which most universities were ill-prepared. At the same time, universities face mounting political pressure over perceptions that the Chinese government exerts undue influence over their decision-making. And as if that weren't enough, tensions between universities and society at large have worsened over issues like freedom of speech, cancel culture, and (a lack of) viewpoint diversity.

With universities experiencing simultaneous financial, pedagogical, and ideological challenges, the sense of crisis on campus is palpable—not that many people have been on campus recently. There is also a sense that change is in the air. More than half of Australia's universities appointed new vice chancellors in 2020 and 2021, an unprecedented churn that seems to have less to do with the pandemic than with a coincidental generational turnover.[1] The first order of business for most of these new leaders will be enterprise bargaining, with the 'eighth round' of union contracts due to be negotiated in 2021 and 2022. Strong pressure for cost cuts will make this round especially contentious. Meanwhile a federal election is due in 2022, and although an election of some kind is almost always due in Australia, the recent politicisation of higher education makes this one more consequential for universities than most.

And then there's the virus. The virus has, as they say, 'changed everything'. The coronavirus emergency forced universities to make dramatic changes to their ordinary organisational practices at breakneck speed. Classes were moved online, courses were canceled, building programs were suspended, and staff were let go. The pandemic also reminded governments (both Commonwealth and state) of the extensive powers they hold over universities and the important duties they have to ensure that universities fulfil their public service missions. Rarely have there been so many government bodies investigating universities for so many different reasons at the same time. Thus at the very moment that universities have been required to demonstrate their adaptability, governments have been reminded of their authority. As a result, universities, until recently ivory tower bastions of organisational conservatism, seem newly open (or vulnerable) to reform.

In the past, government-prompted university reforms have often entailed pro forma compliance without meaningful change. During the pandemic, however, universities actually undertook meaningful change, but without any systematic attempt at reform. With new conditions, new leadership, and either a new or a reinvigorated government all arriving at the very moment the country exits from its coronavirus experience, there has perhaps never been a better occasion for university reform than 2022. The fact that Australia's universities are simultaneously in the midst of multiple crises only adds to the sense of opportunity. Yet while the need for reform is clear to almost everyone, and the time for reform may have at last arrived, the correct direction for reform is not obvious. Australia's universities are large, unwieldy, and (it often seems intentionally) opaque. What's more, nearly all of the major voices in higher education policy debates are deeply invested in their outcomes. It is hard for the public to find disinterested advice on university reform.

Good policy requires good data to light the way toward effective solutions. It cannot be made in the dark. A perennial problem for higher education policymaking is that much of the data that are needed to inform good policy is held by gatekeepers with strong interests in swaying the outcomes of reform—or in preventing reform altogether. Vested interests are everywhere. For university administrators and their trade associations, reform means more government money with less public accountability. For staff unions, reform means permanent lifetime employment for anyone who seeks an academic career. For student unions, reform means free tuition for unlimited degrees, plus a generous stipend. For government agencies, reform is unnecessary, since nothing is more comfortable than business as usual.

All of these groups have historically been economical in their provision of data that might inform public debate, to say the least. That is a problem. Australia has to know much more about its universities and their operations in order to reform its universities, and it needs information without an agenda if it is going to get university reform right. This book provides that disinterested data, supporting policymakers and the public in formulating their own opinions on higher education reform. Where formal data are lacking, this book offers insider insights in their place. That is perhaps inadequate, but it is nonetheless indispensable: the relevant data needed to guide policymaking are often plagued by self-serving lacunae, and it is better to fill them with credible inferences than to allow them to remain strategically empty.

This book also offers disinterested policy advice, clearly presented as advice. Readers will not struggle to distinguish information from opinion. No one is without biases, but whatever biases may underlie this book are at least free from economic, social, organisational, or political interests. The author is an ordinary academic who holds no major leadership roles—past, present, or (as this book makes almost certain) future. The book is thoroughly data-driven, and although it is suffused with a certain moral rectitude, it is scrupulously even-handed. The book is neither pro-government nor anti-government; neither progressive nor conservative; neither focused on the capital cities nor particularly sympathetic to the regions. If the book takes sides at all, it takes the sides of Australia's taxpayers and students: the primary sponsors of the Australian university system, and its primary intended beneficiaries.

The politicians whose decisions will shape the future of Australia's universities cannot be expected to have a detailed knowledge of the inner workings of each institution, never mind the system as a whole. Neither can the members of the public who elect them. The Australian news media do an exceptionally good job of reporting on universities, but their coverage is necessarily episodic and focused on personalities. This book complements press reports by being systematic and impersonal. In fact, not a single person is mentioned throughout the entire book; names are not named, and stories go untold. Australia's journalists are more than capable of fleshing out the human details. This book is about institutional data, the problems they expose, the opportunities they reveal, and the reforms that should follow.

Autonomy without responsibility

Considering that Australia's major universities are all not-for-profit public sector organisations, they are remarkably prone to financial crises. The reasons for this are structural. Funding shortfalls (real or manufactured) are absolutely necessary for institutions that rely on government subsidies to pay their bills: they have to create a perception of crisis in order to convince politicians to prioritise their needs. Unfortunately for the universities, a country's educational choices are highly flexible: a country can buy Oxbridge-style bespoke teaching with individualised tuition, or it can buy American-style mass teaching with thousand-student classrooms. A country can top the international league tables for research, like the United States, or it can lag far behind, like Germany and Japan. There are many paths to national success, and it is not at all clear that having a 'world-class' university system confers any benefits on a country whatsoever.

There are no 'proper' or even 'adequate' levels of university funding. There are only lower and higher levels, and universities have an overwhelming interest in convincing people that existing funding levels are far too low. Dangerously so.

Thus in one sense at least the coronavirus crisis came as a boon to the Australian university system: it put university funding back on the agenda. Until the coronavirus hit, the headline 'crisis' afflicting Australia's universities wasn't the usual funding crisis, but a free speech crisis. In a sector that thrives on crises, that was one crisis that the universities did not want to have. The principle of academic freedom is the foundation of university demands for absolute autonomy in governance and priority-setting, and any suggestion that they themselves restrict the free speech of their staff and students risks undermining their uniquely privileged place in society. Universities would much rather face a financial panic than a moral one. Financial crises always have one obvious solution: more money. Moral crises, by contrast, are much more dangerous: they might elicit calls for increased oversight or systemic reform.

Yet in 2018 and 2019, Australian universities were struggling to counter perceptions that they had lost their moral compass on free speech. The crisis atmosphere was driven by a few high-profile cases of disciplinary actions taken against tenured academics and the broad-based rise of a campus 'cancel culture' that originated overseas but showed signs of spreading to Australia. Worries over rising Chinese government influence only fanned the flames. Taken together, these various concerns added up to a molehill, but not quite a mountain. Public perceptions of a university free speech crisis actually rested on a series of unrelated cases and causes, and there was no major event at the centre of the crisis that critics could point to as representing the essence of the malfeasance they were so keen to assert. But perceptions matter, and Parliament was holding hearings. The press smelled blood.

There may have been no clear centre to the supposed free speech crisis of 2018-2019, but there was an epicentre. That was the controversy over the Ramsay Centre for Western Civilisation. At a time when universities claimed to be experiencing a funding crisis (which is to say: at any time), the Ramsay Centre proposed to rescue the humanities with a massive cash infusion. You would think it would be easy to give some of Australia's top universities $150 million to support their humanities departments, but you would think wrong. Academics doggedly opposed the Ramsay grants, many of them equating 'Western civilisation' with 'racism' and 'fascism'. The Ramsay Centre failed to reach funding agreements with the ANU and Sydney, and had to settle for much less prestigious programs at ACU and Wollongong. A third Ramsay-funded program at Queensland also proved controversial, though university management successfully overcame staff opposition to push it through.

Whatever academics may have thought about the Ramsay Centre's proposed governance model for the programs it offered to fund, the implication that traditional Western values had no place in the twenty-first century university was not a good look. Nonetheless, the deals at ANU and Sydney ultimately ran aground on the governance model, not the politics. The ANU's vice chancellor stated unequivocally that "we took our decision for no other reason than the Centre's continued demands for control over the program were inconsistent with the University's academic autonomy".[2] Sydney's wrote that "the one thing that has never been on the table was compromising our academic freedom and integrity", implying that the Ramsay Centre wanted to infringe on both.[3] These quotes came from Ramsay Centre's managerial boosters. The academic critics were much, much harsher.

The Ramsay Centre's great transgression (in the eyes of these university leaders) was to insist on maintaining a degree of ongoing supervision over how its money would be spent. The Centre apparently demanded a seat on academic hiring committees and veto power over the curriculum to be taught in its name. It fussed over the names of the degrees to be offered, preferring 'Western civilisation' to 'Western civilisation studies'. It insisted on structuring its support in the form of fixed-term, renewable grants instead of offering to provide fully-funded, perpetual endowments. It solicited proposals in the spirit of a patron seeking clients, not that of donor offering benefices. It had an agenda. To quote the emphatic words of its most controversial board member, the Ramsay Centre wanted to ensure that the programs it funded were "not merely *about* Western civilisation but *in favour* of it".[4]

To institutions accustomed to receiving billions of dollars in student fees and Commonwealth subsidies with few strings attached, the Ramsay Centre attitude was anathema. The Ramsay Centre demanded accountability. Students are in no position to hold universities to account. It is almost impossible for students to meaningfully evaluate universities and make informed decisions about where to spend their tuition money. Nor does the Commonwealth do much to discipline the universities it funds. It generally allows public universities to self-certify the quality of their degrees; it makes research grants on the strength of professors' evaluations of their colleagues' proposals. As long as a sufficient number of students receive degrees and the staff unions don't make too much noise, students accept the status quo as a fait accompli and most governments are satisfied to let the universities govern themselves.

The reluctance of several prestigious universities to accept funding from the Ramsay Centre brought university governance out of the shadows and exposed universities' prized autonomy to public scrutiny. It was pointed out that universities routinely accepted money from unsavoury individuals and foreign governments, but were wary of getting involved with an Australian foundation that had two retired prime ministers on its board. That was all too true—but only half of the truth. Unlike the Ramsay Centre, unsavoury individuals and governments typically do not seek formal input into the operation of the programs they fund. Shadowy influencers don't challenge the authority of vice chancellors; they operate through the authority of vice chancellors. They offer discretionary funds for pet projects and demand little in the way of concrete deliverables or auditable results. They are generally interested in negative outcomes, not positive ones. They aren't buying university speech. They're buying university self-censorship.

Thus the free speech crisis fizzled out for a lack of evidence. If there is a free speech crisis at Australian universities, it's not because people are being fired for their political views. It's because intellectually challenging people are not being hired in the first place. Events are not being canceled; they are simply not being held. Books are not being written. Papers are not being published. Degree courses—in particular, humanities degree courses—are no longer being offered.[5] The 2019 Report of the Independent Review of Freedom of Speech in Australian Higher Education Providers (known after its chairman as the "French Review") took 300 pages to conclude that "claims of a freedom of speech crisis on Australian campuses are not substantiated".[6] They might have saved the ink: you can't substantiate a black hole. Western civilisation isn't falling in battle with the forces of evil. It is dying in the darkness of neglect.

If there is a crisis in the Australian university system, it is not primarily a financial crisis. Nor is it, properly speaking, a free speech crisis. It is a moral crisis. It is a breach of faith, a betrayal of the public trust. Australia's universities are suffering a collective crisis of responsibility, clinging desperately to the institutional autonomy guaranteed by government financial support while self-indulgently pursuing their own parochial goals. Wide-ranging institutional autonomy should be accompanied by a thoroughgoing sense of institutional responsibility, especially when that autonomy is purchased at public expense. Australia's universities have embraced their autonomy, but rejected the responsibilities that go along with it. The solution, however, is not more government control. The solution is for Australia's governments to put in place mechanisms that hold universities accountable for exercising their autonomy in the public interest.

Australia's higher education landscape

Today's universities are the direct lineal descendants of the Medieval universities of western Europe. Politically correct authors often place the first universities in India, China, or the Arab world, but these accounts are more than a little disingenuous. Certainly, educational institutions involved in both teaching and research stretch back to ancient history, but these institutions were not the ancestors of today's universities. There is a straight line of organic development from Medieval European universities, via England's Oxford University, to the institutional structure of Australia's universities nearly 1000 years later. Perhaps most importantly, the basic set of degrees conferred in Medieval Europe—Bachelor of Arts, Master of Arts, Doctor of Medicine, Doctor of Law, Doctor of Theology, and Doctor of Philosophy—recognisably form the core of the myriad degrees offered today.

Universities have long been the guardians of a specifically Western civilisation. Even non-Western universities typically organise their curriculums along historically Western models. The principle that universities should be autonomous is also distinctively Western. It stands in stark contrast to the organisation of K-12 schooling, which is thoroughly embedded in government administration and control. Like many countries, Western and non-Western alike, Australia has a national curriculum for K-12 schooling that even non-state schools have to follow. Yet it is hard to imagine any country adopting a university-level national curriculum; only China comes close. In Australia, universities have extensive autonomy to design their own curriculums, but they are not the only institutions offering university-level degrees, and the level of government oversight differs across institutions.

Australian university degrees (and courses that contribute credits toward university degrees) are offered by a mix of 'higher education providers' overseen by the Tertiary Education Quality and Standards Agency (TEQSA), an independent regulatory body reporting to the Minister for Education. As of June 30, 2021 (the baseline date for the analyses presented in this book), there were 186 higher education providers actively registered to offer courses in Australia. Of these, 40 were classified as 'Australian universities'. This group included 37 public universities, 1 large private university (Notre Dame), 1 small private university (Bond), and 1 for-profit university (Torrens). Also operating in Australia were 3 private quasi-university institutions: 1 'overseas university' (CMU), 1 'Australian university college' (Avondale), and 1 'Australian university of specialisation' (Divinity). The classifications of Australian higher education providers as of June 2021 are summarised in Table 1.

As of June 30, there were a total of 55 institutions in Australia that were either self-accrediting or partially self-accrediting. A further 131 higher education providers also offered higher education courses that were accredited directly by TEQSA. In July 2021 there were several changes to TEQSA's lists, with Avondale University College and the University of Divinity becoming 'Australian universities' while AFTRS, the Moore Theological College, and NIDA were upgraded to 'university

Table 1. Governance of Australian Higher Education Providers (as of June 2021)

Institution	Ownership	HESA Table	TEQSA Classification	Self-Accrediting?	Notes
ACU	Public	A	Australian University	Yes	
Adelaide	Public	A	Australian University	Yes	Group of 8
ANU	Public	A	Australian University	Yes	Group of 8
Canberra	Public	A	Australian University	Yes	
CDU	Public	A	Australian University	Yes	Dual sector
CQU	Public	A	Australian University	Yes	Dual sector
CSU	Public	A	Australian University	Yes	
Curtin	Public	A	Australian University	Yes	
Deakin	Public	A	Australian University	Yes	
ECU	Public	A	Australian University	Yes	
Federation	Public	A	Australian University	Yes	Dual sector
Flinders	Public	A	Australian University	Yes	
Griffith	Public	A	Australian University	Yes	
JCU	Public	A	Australian University	Yes	
La Trobe	Public	A	Australian University	Yes	
Macquarie	Public	A	Australian University	Yes	
Melbourne	Public	A	Australian University	Yes	Group of 8
Monash	Public	A	Australian University	Yes	Group of 8
Murdoch	Public	A	Australian University	Yes	
Newcastle	Public	A	Australian University	Yes	
Notre Dame	Private	A	Australian University	Yes	
Queensland	Public	A	Australian University	Yes	Group of 8
QUT	Public	A	Australian University	Yes	
RMIT	Public	A	Australian University	Yes	Dual sector
SCU	Public	A	Australian University	Yes	
Swinburne	Public	A	Australian University	Yes	Dual sector
Sydney	Public	A	Australian University	Yes	Group of 8
Tasmania	Public	A	Australian University	Yes	
UNE	Public	A	Australian University	Yes	
UNISA	Public	A	Australian University	Yes	
UNSW	Public	A	Australian University	Yes	Group of 8
USC	Public	A	Australian University	Yes	
USQ	Public	A	Australian University	Yes	
UTS	Public	A	Australian University	Yes	
UWA	Public	A	Australian University	Yes	Group of 8
Victoria	Public	A	Australian University	Yes	Dual sector
Wollongong	Public	A	Australian University	Yes	
WSU	Public	A	Australian University	Yes	
Batchelor	Public	A	Higher Education Provider	Partial	Dual sector
Bond	Private	B	Australian University	Yes	
Torrens	For-profit	B	Australian University	Yes	
Divinity	Private	B	Aus. Univ. of Specialisation	Partial	
CMU	Private	C	Overseas University	Yes	
Avondale	Private	N/A	Australian Univ. College	Yes	Dual sector
ACAP	For-profit	N/A	Higher Education Provider	Partial	Dual sector
ACT	Private	N/A	Higher Education Provider	Partial	
AFTRS	For-profit	N/A	Higher Education Provider	Yes	
Alphacrucis	Private	N/A	Higher Education Provider	Partial	Dual sector
COLA	Private	N/A	Higher Education Provider	Partial	
Excelsia	Private	N/A	Higher Education Provider	Partial	
Moore	Private	N/A	Higher Education Provider	Yes	
NIDA	Private	N/A	Higher Education Provider	Partial	Dual sector
SAE/Qantm	For-profit	N/A	Higher Education Provider	Partial	Dual sector
SCD	Private	N/A	Higher Education Provider	Partial	
Top/ANIMC	For-profit	N/A	Higher Education Provider	Partial	
+ 131 others	Various	N/A	Higher Education Providers	No	

college' status. With the exception of the University of Divinity and NIDA, all of Australia's university-like institutions are self-accrediting, which means that they can offer courses on their own cognisance (i.e., without specific approval from TEQSA). The University of Divinity and NIDA are only partially self-accrediting, meaning that they can self-accredit only specified courses. Several other higher education providers are also partially self-accrediting, including a mix of public, private, and for-profit institutions.

Higher education courses include, but are not limited to, the traditional degrees that have historically formed the core offerings of universities. A course of study is defined by TEQSA as a "coherent sequence of units of study leading to an award of a qualification" that may or may not be a degree.[7] Qualifications are sorted according to the Australian Qualifications Framework (AQF), a 10-level scheme ranking qualifications from vocational certificates (I, II, III, and IV) through to higher education diplomas and degrees. Higher education starts with the diploma (Level 5) and the advanced diploma or associate degree (Level 6). Diplomas and associate degrees are not traditional university courses, but are still considered higher education qualifications, and in many cases the units taken in pursuit of these qualifications can be counted for credit toward traditional university degrees. Bachelor degrees (Level 7), honours, graduate certificates, and graduate diplomas (Level 8), master degrees (Level 9), and doctorates (Level 10) round out the AQF.

Although on June 30 the university sector proper consisted of only 40 universities and 3 quasi-universities, there were 186 higher education providers that either offered or contributed units that can be counted toward traditional university degrees. There were also 6 dual-sector universities (CDU, CQU, Federation, RMIT, Swinburne, and Victoria) that offered vocational certificates in addition to higher education diplomas and degrees. Many non-university higher education providers also award both higher education qualifications and vocational certificates. The higher education sector as a whole is thus quite complicated. Nonetheless, most policy discussion focuses on the 37 public universities, plus the private University of Notre Dame. This group became even more cohesive in June 2021, when the Higher Education Support Act (HESA) was amended to include Notre Dame among the 'Table A' institutions eligible for public support. Table A also includes the Batchelor Institute of Indigenous Tertiary Education, a public higher education provider that is partially self-accrediting but is not a university.

In addition to the 39 Table A higher education providers, the HESA also names 3 'Table B' institutions (Bond, Divinity, and Torrens) and one 'Table C' institution (CMU). Table A institutions are eligible for all government grant programs, and their students can access commonwealth supported places with HECS-HELP support. Table B institutions are eligible for some government grant programs, and their students can access commonwealth supported places only in national priority fields. Table C institutions, a category created to accommodate Australian branch campuses of foreign universities, are generally ineligible for government grant programs, and their students can access commonwealth supported places only in national priority fields. Students at all HESA listed institutions are eligible for FEE-HELP, OS-HELP, and SA-HELP loans, as are students at most other higher education providers.

As a result of all this complexity, Australia's higher education landscape looks very different from the student perspective than it does from that of the university administrator, education analyst, or government policymaker. The public discourse surrounding higher education tends to focus on the major state-supported institutions that teach nearly all of Australia's high-achieving school graduates—and ignore the rest of the system. Since these relatively more prestigious institutions receive the bulk of the Commonwealth's public funding, it makes sense for policy analysis to focus on them. But it is important to remember that they are enmeshed in a wider system that offers students many pathways to traditional university degrees. This book is mainly concerned with the reform of Australia's universities, but seen from the student perspective, universities are only a part (though by far the most important part) of the overall higher education landscape.

Defining the university sector

Although there were 186 higher education providers in Australia (as of June 30, 2021) that were empowered to contribute in some way toward helping students eventually receive university-style degrees, most of the student load is borne by the 39 Table A providers (the 37 public universities, Notre Dame, and Batchelor). According to 2019 data from the Department of Education, Skills and Employment (DESE), these institutions account for 91.4% of the equivalent full-time student load (EFTSL) taught by all higher education providers combined, and 94.4% of the domestic student EFTSL. Even when it comes to international students, they still account for 85.8% of EFTSL. These figures are only slightly lower when considering individual students by headcount instead of EFTSL, which weights students according to the number of credits for which they are enrolled.

The Table A institutions thus cover over 90% of the higher education sector, and an even greater proportion of that part of the sector that is of greatest public policy interest. They are also the 39 institutions that receive direct government support via the Commonwealth Grant Scheme. That further increases their policy relevance. It also means that additional financial data are readily available for these institutions via the DESE's annual finance publications. Compared to the other Table A institutions, Batchelor is extremely small (enrolling only 12 higher education students in 2019, accounting for 10 EFTSL), and in any case it is not a university. It can effectively be ignored when examining system-wide revenue or student statistics with a negligible effect on the interpretability of the national statistics. But the other 38 form the heart of Australia's university system.

The peak trade body for Australian universities, Universities Australia, includes as members the 37 public universities, Notre Dame, and Bond. Although Bond is a member, and its 2019 EFTSL of 5908 gives it a substantial student load, it has historically taken a different trajectory from the main body of the university sector. The other Table B universities, Torrens (10,723 EFTSL) and Divinity (660 EFTSL) are not members of Universities Australia. Both Table A and Table B institutions are required to submit annual mission based compacts to DESE, so there is a case for including all of them in a study of the university system. But many university statistics are available only for the 39 Table A institutions. Ideally, sector-wide data and analyses might include all Table A and Table B institutions, or focus only on the 39 members of Universities Australia, or cover only universities, but practically speaking the regular reporting of data for Table A institutions and their access to Commonwealth Grant Scheme funding make Table A the obvious focus list for this book.

It is important to keep in mind that Table A does not cover the entire university sector, never mind the higher education sector. Many students, particularly those from the least advantaged family backgrounds, may first enter the sector through non-university higher education providers. Enrolment statistics are available for some of these providers, but in most statistics they are aggregated at the state level. Moreover, financial statistics for these providers are generally not made public. Many higher education providers are private businesses. For example, Torrens University is owned by the American company Strategic Education Inc. Although private providers fall outside the scope of this book, they are likely to form an ever more important component of Australia's higher education landscape.

And a new competitor is visible on the horizon, one that lies completely outside the framework of Australian regulation. American online universities and educational technology companies have gone global, and there is no reason to expect that Australian students will not enrol in their programs. Presumably, many already have. After all, pandemic measures have left tens of thousands of students at Australian universities enrolled offshore; if international students can study online in Australia, why shouldn't Australian students study online in the United States? Highly subsidised courses are likely to keep the bulk of Australian domestic undergraduate students at home, but it is likely that many Australian professionals are already pursuing online postgraduate coursework degrees at top American universities. In the absence of any statistics on this emerging trend, its implications can only be hinted at. But Australian universities ignore this international online competition at their peril.

Finally, in addition to its main focus on the 39 Table A institutions, this book shines a spotlight on Australia's Group of Eight (Go8) research-intensive universities. The Go8's member universities are Adelaide, ANU, Melbourne, Monash,

Queensland, Sydney, UNSW, and UWA. The Go8 includes all eight Australian universities that place in the top 100 on any of the major international rankings systems. The Go8 also accounted for 35.0% of Australia's total international student EFTSL in 2019, and 40.8% of the international EFTSL of Table A institutions. When the Commonwealth government required universities to register their contracts with foreign governments and some (primarily Chinese) foreign universities under the Foreign Arrangements Scheme, roughly two-thirds of the submissions came from Go8 universities.[8] Six of the Go8 universities host Confucius Institutes funded by the Chinese government, accounting for half of Australia's total.

The Go8 is important not only for its international connections, but also for its outsized influence on the government's strategic thinking. It commissions a substantial amount of policy-relevant research and presents itself as "a leader in influencing the development and delivery of long-term sustainable national higher education and research policy".[9] Although the Commonwealth sets higher education policy (and provides the bulk of the higher education funding) for all students across the entire university system, the prominence of the Go8 in policy debates raises the risk that the government may put disproportionate weight on the needs of Go8 universities. Other groups of Australian universities have been formed as shifting counterweights to the Go8 (e.g., Australian Technology Network, Innovative Research Universities, Regional Universities Network), but they hardly figure in national higher education debates. Thus this book highlights only the Go8 universities within its wider coverage of the Table A institutions as a whole.

Mission and policy

When it comes to imagining the post-pandemic future of Australia's university system, the availability of good data is only an input, a necessary condition for policy formation. Another, even more important input is mission: knowing what we want from our universities. Mission is even more contentious than data, but it is not merely a matter of opinion. Whatever individual Australians might think their universities should deliver, and whatever the student organisations, staff unions, and trade associations may think, the universities themselves have gone on record—the official, statutory record—with statements of their missions. All HESA Table A and Table B institutions must file annual 'mission based compacts' with the DESE. These constitute commitments to the Commonwealth, and thus ultimately to the Australian public.

The mission based compacts mandated under the HESA are formulaic, but not prescriptive. The law requires universities to summarise their overall missions and their strategies for teaching, research, industry engagement, and improving equal opportunity, but only in the most general terms. The universities are left free to interpret these requirements as they see fit. The Minister for Education does not have to accept a university's proposed compact, but the compacts are clearly written by the universities, not by the minister. Reading them, it is clear that they are not boilerplate: they exude individuality, and can reasonably be taken to represent voluntary expressions of each university's self-understanding and ambitions.

The mission statements contained in these compacts are brief, but evocative. In its 2020 compact, the Australian National University says it will "focus on providing the nation with world-class research and education capacity that will contribute to Australia's economy, society and engagement with our world". Note the explicit focus on capacity, not on research and education as such: it implies a commitment to institution-building beyond the immediate deliverables of teaching and research. The university also expresses its intention "to provide a student experience that is comparable with the world's best". The Australian Catholic University, by contrast, summarises its mission as "the pursuit of knowledge, the dignity of the human person and the common good". It wants to "to inspire and equip students to make a difference—to be ethical leaders, to act empathetically and to give back to society". These student-centred ambitions clearly differentiate it from ANU.

One might expect university mission statements to be generic and boring, and they are. But they can also be revealing. For example, the University of Melbourne touts that it "will embrace the possibilities of digital evolution" that "will combine the best of blended learning with time spent alongside teachers and peers", while the University of Newcastle pledges that "all undergraduate programs will feature work-integrated learning opportunities". It is not hard to see from this that while Melbourne intends to push forward with e-learning after the pandemic, Newcastle is more focused on job placement. The University of Adelaide's bullet-pointed mission statement, filed in the midst of a leadership crisis, looks forward to a weighty "215t Century" (sic) with text carelessly lifted directly from its 2019 strategic plan. Across the street, the University of South Australia, much like Newcastle, focuses on "educating global learners from all backgrounds for the professions of the future". Fair enough.

The HESA mandates that all Table A and Table B institutions "must have a policy that upholds freedom of speech and academic freedom", and so it comes as no surprise that all of them address this in their mission based compacts. Most embrace the mandate, with many emphasising that various formulations of intellectual freedom are enshrined both in their institutional policies and in their enterprise agreements. The Batchelor Institute of Indigenous Tertiary Education, somewhat amusingly, devotes nearly half of its mission statement to explaining why it has not adopted the model code proposed by the French Review. Its current code of conduct prohibits staff from publicly criticizing the institute—a provision that is surely inconsistent with the spirit of the review, to say the least.[10]

Other aspects of the mission statements are more murky. For example, despite the constant drumbeat of public claims that education is Australia's third largest export, only one university mentions the goal of generating services export revenues: the University of Sydney. Strangely, this occurs in its section on 'equity', which is supposed to focus on "the provider's strategies for improving equality of opportunity in higher education". In the course of underlining its equity commitment to the development of western Sydney, the university estimates that "over the next 30 years ... [it] will create ... $15 billion in exports" in the region. This goal, as expressed in the document, is specific to its planned Parramatta/Westmead Campus. No other university even mentions the possibility that the potential to generate export revenues might form part of its institutional mission. The very word 'export' only ever appears in the context of support for industry or compliance with defence export controls

Similarly, China gets short shrift across the entire sector. Only 5 institutions even mention China at all in their mission-based compacts: Monash and Notre Dame in the context of study abroad programs (for Australian students to go to China), Adelaide and QUT in the context of institutional partnerships with Chinese universities, and Macquarie in the context of its new Master of Research degree, which seems to be tailored for Chinese students who need additional preparation before undertaking doctoral studies in Australia. And that's it. Not a single university mentions China in its broad mission statement, despite the extraordinary attention devoted to China ties by Australian universities, and by Go8 vice chancellors in particular. Given how many Australian universities have China strategies, China centres, China recruitment agents, and even Chinese language websites, it is a bit shocking that not a single one mentions China in its overarching mission statement.

Given that Australian universities now draw roughly 1 in every 10 of their students from China, it seems that China should merit a more prominent place. For those capital city universities at which Chinese students make up more than a quarter of their student bodies, surely the education of Chinese students should form a major element of their educational missions. The reticence of Australian universities on this topic is more telling than any boilerplate language could be. If the Commonwealth is serious about holding universities accountable for fulfilling the obligations they make in their mission compacts, it might consider requiring universities to align their behavior (and their executive compensation terms) with their stated missions. In particular, it seems reasonable to expect that vice chancellor performance incentives should be aligned with universities' self-professed missions. It would be interesting to discover the extent to which they really are.

* * *

What are Australia's universities? Legally, they are the 42 universities now classified by TEQSA as Australian universities, plus perhaps the various quasi-universities. More broadly, all of

Australia's 186 active higher education providers are licensed to contribute units of study to the university system. More broadly still, the university system might be taken to include the myriad schools, research institutes, and even foreign universities that in one way or another contribute toward the missions of educating Australian bachelor, master, and doctoral students. More practically, Australia's university system is probably best understood as consisting of the 39 higher education providers named in Table A of the HESA. But in the end, universities are all about the students, the courses they pursue, and the degrees they earn. The system exists to serve the students, not the other way around.

When New South Wales set up the University of Sydney in 1850, it did so "for the purpose of ascertaining by means of examination, the persons who shall acquire proficiency in literature, science and art, and of rewarding them by academical degrees".[11] Similarly, the University of Melbourne was constituted in 1853 "to promote sound learning in the colony of Victoria".[12] Today, with rare exceptions, the Commonwealth funds student places, not staff places. Most university research is funded, not for its own sake, but on the argument that university students should be taught by people who are themselves active in research. That traditional model of the research university is reflected in staff enterprise agreements that ordinarily stipulate that academic staff should engage in teaching, research, and service activities on the basis of a 40-40-20 relative allocation of time.

University and government reactions to the coronavirus crisis have underlined just how far universities have strayed from their core statutory missions.[13] No state legislature ever chartered a university for the purpose of generating export revenue, or to undertake research in isolation from teaching.

Yet reading from the press releases of Australian university trade organisations, it can sometimes seem as if teaching is the least of their members' activities.[14] Universities have taken it on themselves to behave as teaching-funded research institutes, providing education services (including education exports) primarily as a means to generate revenue to support research. When that revenue was threatened, they didn't scale back their research ambitions to a level commensurate with their reduced student numbers. They cut teaching staff, and turned to the government for a research bailout.

Research is where the prestige is; it's what universities are ranked on, and what they prefer to be ranked on. But unlike the Commonwealth Scientific and Industrial Research Organisation (CSIRO), Australia's universities have not been charged by the government with meeting Australia's research needs. Indeed, they do not generally pursue research in line with the government's priorities at all. Quite the contrary: they demand autonomy, and extol the virtues of academic freedom. Ministerial intervention in research funding decisions is decried as 'political interference', not welcomed as valued feedback from the democratically elected representatives of the people. In one sense, that's reasonable enough. Academic freedom really is essential—for teaching institutions. It's worth remembering that no one expects CSIRO to set its own research priorities.

La Trobe University's stated mission probably best captures the purpose of a university: "advancing knowledge and learning to shape the future of our students and communities". Related themes are peppered throughout other universities' statutory compacts: quality teaching, the employability of graduates, the importance of community, and of course research excellence. There is also a lot of language about being 'global' and 'sustainable', but this is mere window dressing. The first should be taken for granted in this as in any century: as the University of Sydney's much-maligned Latin motto says: *sidere mens eadem mutato*. The universities' commitment to the second will be severely tested when travel restrictions are lifted and we discover whether or not academics are content to continue attending international conferences online. The northern hemisphere beckons.

Universities and the academics who work in them like to wax eloquent about global responsibilities while disclaiming any direct accountability to the actual communities that host and fund them. This book offers a practical foundation for policy reform based on an old-fashioned vision of the university as an institution devoted to teaching, research, and service—to the community. Collectively, the 42 university compacts use variations of the word 'community' 756 times, and although it is often used self-referentially, most universities also make explicit commitments to the geographical communities they serve. The book thus focuses on universities' teaching, research, and service in the context of Australian communities, and the Australian community writ large. More than one-third of the students who learn on (and increasingly off) Australia's university campuses may be foreign, but the universities themselves are, after all, Australian.

CHAPTER 2

Are Australia's universities 'underfunded'?

"We cannot keep cutting back on funding for university education", especially considering that Australian universities have suffered from "disturbingly low levels of public investment" for a decade or more.[15] "Government funding is totally inadequate".[16] Australia's "universities have been brought to their knees" by budget cuts.[17] The situation is so serious that deficiencies "in research funding in Australia represent a sovereign risk to the nation".[18] Australia's universities have been "repeatedly treated by Government as a cash cow to be milked for budget cuts".[19] They have been "left to bleed to death" during the coronavirus pandemic.[20] Indeed, "the government is slashing university funding to the lowest levels in decades".[21] As a result, "the funding universities receive for domestic undergraduates is insufficient to provide them a world-class education. Research is also underfunded. This has left universities with no choice but to enrol large numbers of foreign students, paying market prices for their education".[22]

The idea that Australia's universities face chronic underfunding and relentless government budget cuts is a timeless trope. But is it true? The media has largely accepted the universities' self-serving narrative that they were 'forced' to turn to international students for their very survival after repeated government budget cuts, then were blindsided by arbitrary border closures and cruelly denied government support when the coronavirus pandemic hit. That sounds credible on first reading, but it can be hard to square the rapidly rising university executive remuneration of the last two decades with a narrative of chronic austerity. That the coronavirus pandemic caused severe financial stress seems more certain, but most universities survived the first year of the crisis with their finances curiously intact. Had they used the surpluses generated in past years to establish appropriate financial reserves, they might hardly have felt the crisis at all.[23]

Data on revenues at Go8 universities, collated from their annual reports, are summarised in Table 2. All data in this and all subsequent tables throughout this book are presented in real 2020 Australian dollars, adjusted for inflation. The Go8 as a whole suffered a revenue decline of 5.59% in 2020. The only Go8 university to manage a (real) revenue increase was Sydney, which actually increased its international student fee revenue despite coronavirus-related travel restrictions. Its accounts suggest that it more than made up for declining international undergraduate enrolments by convincing students to stay another year or two to complete a postgraduate degree. Adelaide very nearly kept revenues constant, while Queensland experienced only a modest decline. Melbourne, ANU, UWA, and Monash were harder-hit, but more than half of Melbourne's revenue decline, nearly three-quarters of ANU's, more than three-quarters of UWA's, and more than 90% of Monash's were due to lower investment returns. These can hardly be blamed on government policy.

The ANU and Melbourne would have experienced severe financial stress in 2020 even if international student revenues

Table 2. Selected Go8 revenue changes, 2019-2020 ($ 2020)

University	Total revenue		Aus. government		Investment income		Int'l student fees	
	Change	Percent	Change	Percent	Change	Percent	Change	Percent
Adelaide	-$3,104,000	-0.32%	$8,397,000	2.87%	-$26,714,000	-50.49%	-$2,739,000	-1.07%
ANU	-$247,439,000	-16.02%	$8,830,000	1.31%	-$174,301,000	-73.93%	-$84,271,000	-25.67%
Melbourne	-$213,705,000	-7.43%	$1,877,000	0.18%	-$108,763,000	-48.70%	-$66,802,000	-7.32%
Monash	-$116,726,000	-4.14%	$17,227,000	1.54%	-$88,753,000	-59.91%	-$33,588,000	-3.35%
Queensland	-$60,707,000	-2.88%	-$3,528,000	-0.37%	-$25,962,000	-67.07%	-$34,391,000	-5.19%
Sydney	$14,820,000	0.56%	-$3,462,000	-0.36%	-$12,173,000	-10.11%	$34,226,000	3.20%
UNSW	-$193,102,000	-8.20%	$39,997,000	3.88%	-$42,751,000	-48.47%	-$102,716,000	-13.27%
UWA	-$97,712,000	-9.16%	-$12,877,000	-2.56%	-$70,960,000	-54.79%	-$12,616,000	-8.36%
Go8 total	-$917,675,000	-5.59%	$56,461,000	0.86%	-$550,376,000	-53.07%	-$302,897,000	-5.87%

had remained constant at 2019 levels, although of course their declines in international student fees didn't help. The only other Go8 university that seems to have been seriously harmed by coronavirus border closures is UNSW, with more than half of its $173 million revenue decline being attributable to a fall in international student fee revenue. For the Go8 as a whole, revenue declines due to falling investment returns were almost twice as high as revenue declines from falling international student numbers. In relative terms, the investment revenue declines were catastrophic. Investment returns declined 53% across the Go8 as a whole and by 48% or more at every Go8 university except Sydney. International student fee revenue was positively stable by comparison.

Across the rest of the sector, the story is similar. Only four non-Go8 universities have international student enrolments that are comparable to those of Go8 universities: RMIT, Wollongong, Victoria, and UTS. They experienced real revenue declines ranging from 4.4% (UTS) to 10.5% (Wollongong). As with many of the hardest hit Go8 universities, Wollongong suffered more from declining investment revenue than from the fall in international student fees. All four universities benefitted from higher levels of government support in 2020 compared to 2019. At the other end of the international exposure spectrum, revenue was essentially flat at UNE, down slightly at ACU, and up 4.5% at USQ. Revenue was down significantly at WSU and Newcastle—both almost entirely due to declines in investment revenue.

The coronavirus crisis did not end in 2020, and future revenue declines are inevitable as reduced international student intakes in 2020 and 2021 (and beyond?) work their way through the system. Nonetheless, two broad trends are clear. First, a large portion of the most serious revenue declines experienced by Australian universities in 2020 can be traced to either risky or unfortunate investments. This is not only true for the Go8, but for other universities as well.[24] In a year when the ASX ended almost even and superannuation funds avoided systemic losses, critics might rightly ask why Australian university investment portfolios performed so poorly.[25] In the United States, where university investments are much more transparently reported, the average endowment fund gained 2% in 2019-2020 and an impressive 27% in 2020-2021.[26] It would seem that Australian university investment managers have much to answer for.

Second, government financial support for Australia's universities held firm through the pandemic. Much has been made of the fact that the government set the rules for its JobKeeper pandemic relief program in ways that excluded Commonwealth-supported universities.[27] These issues were purely technical: unlike private companies, charities, or even private universities, public universities do not generate revenues year-round, but receive the bulk of their payments on specific days when government grants are processed. Thus while other organisations were allowed to qualify for JobKeeper on the basis of depressed revenues in any given month or quarter, public universities were required to show a revenue fall for a six-month period—i.e., a full semester. This was not, as some would have it, the "final twist of the knife" for universities.[28] It was an entirely appropriate policy tweak made to adjust for the idiosyncrasies of university accounting.

Australia can and should have a reasoned debate on the appropriate level of government support for public universities. But the steady drumbeat of dire warnings delivered by the university sector, uncritically amplified by a credulous media that lacks any alternative source of authoritative information, poorly serves the country and its taxpayers. University finances are so opaque (and government funding is so complex) that it is nearly impossible for anyone outside the system to properly evaluate it. The constraints imposed by a relative lack of publicly available data make it even more difficult to understand university financing in Australia than elsewhere. Nonetheless, some broad trends and patterns can be discerned that illustrate how the Australian university system operates—and reveal the mendacity that underlies much of the received wisdom about Australian university funding.

International funding comparisons

It is difficult to place a monetary value on education. It is possible to estimate the average lifetime earnings boost provided by degree, but such analyses are inevitably backward-looking, and in any case ignore the many non-monetary rewards of higher education. Thus it is impossible to determine the economically appropriate level of public funding for higher education, since without knowing the true value of a degree, it is impossible to determine exactly how much it is reasonable to pay for it. Even studies that attempt to establish the subjective value of a degree to the student (i.e., the customer) offer little guidance as to how much of the cost should be picked up by the public (i.e., the taxpayer). On top of all these difficulties, many argue that universities generate 'positive externalities' for society that extend beyond the degrees they confer: for example, the value of having a national pool of pandemic experts. For these reasons and many more, university funding is more a matter of judgment than analysis, more political than actuarial.

As with most public services, it is always possible to spend more money on higher education. The art comes in knowing where to draw the line. One way to draw the line is benchmarking to the policies and experiences of other countries. The standard (indeed the only) international university finance dataset is that published by the OECD, based on national data reported by three dozen (or so) rich and middle-income countries. These data are often cited to claim that Australian university funding is woefully inadequate. According to the OECD, Australia spends 38.2% less per student on 'tertiary education' (which combines higher education and vocational education) than the United States, and 27.4% less than the United Kingdom, which sounds like sure prima facie evidence of underfunding. But the very same table shows Australian universities spend a whopping 56.5% more per student EFTSL on research than US universities, and 4.6% more than UK universities.[29] By that metric, Australian university research is extraordinarily overfunded.

It's hard to believe that Australian university researchers are rich beyond the wildest dreams of their American counterparts, so that particular OECD comparison is never brought up by the university unions or trade associations. Instead, they prefer to focus on one particular OECD metric: 'public investment'. By this they mean government spending, whereas the figures cited above incorporate funding from all sources. According to the NTEU, public investment figures show "Australia's public investment in higher education being the second lowest in the OECD".[30] Universities Australia confirms that "Australia's public investment in tertiary institutions as a share of GDP was amongst the lowest in the OECD".[31] The Go8 is even more shrill: "for a government enamoured of OECD statistics it is worth noting that for the latest available figures Australia finished 27 out of 32 countries for public investment in tertiary education".[32] That sounds pretty conclusive.

In reality, it's nothing more than deceptive cherry-picking. In each case, the organisations single out the direct support provided by governments to universities, ignoring the total support figures that sit just a few columns to the left. The direct support figures include only government grants to educational institutions, and exclude Commonwealth funding delivered via HECS-HELP, FEE-HELP, and other per-student forms of support.[33] The most recent OECD figure for Australia's total public spending on tertiary education through all forms of support is 1.1% of GDP, which places Australia just above the OECD and European Union averages of 1.0% and exactly at the median among all OECD countries.[34] Since Australia has one of the higher levels of GDP per capita in the OECD, the absolute level of Australian government support for education is well above that in most OECD countries.

It is extraordinarily difficult to make meaningful international comparisons of university finances because the structures of university systems differ wildly across countries. According to OECD data, total tertiary education spending per student (EFTSL) in Australia from all sources (including tuition payments) is the eighth highest in the OECD, and almost tied with the Netherlands for seventh.[35] Canada, Luxembourg, Norway, Sweden, the US, and the UK spend more; everyone else spends less. Wherever the money comes from—government, students, grants, loans, everything—Australian tertiary education providers get more of it per student than most of their competitors across the OECD, and are in the middle of the pack among relatively wealthy peer countries.

Even these rough-cut figures do not capture the full complexity of the situation. For example, Australia has a large number of private vocational education and training (VET) providers. Their students are included in the OECD's count of Australian tertiary student numbers, but they have relatively low revenues per student and receive virtually no government research support. They in effect drag down Australia's per-student spending levels compared to, say, the United States, where the VET sector is relatively much smaller. Such complexities do not make the headlines, but they must be taken into account in order to meaningfully interpret the data. University trade associations should be well aware of them. Their decision not to acknowledge the complexities of OECD data in their funding comparisons says much about the character of their constant demands for increased government support.

Revenue sources of Australian universities

While there may be no such thing as a 'correct' funding level for universities, the near-universal claims of chronic underfunding must be taken with a very large grain of salt. It is hard to believe that a university system that has been as underfunded as Australia's claims to be, for as long as it claims to have been, could even survive, never mind thrive. But by most outcome measures, Australia's universities are at or near peak performance. For example, the industry magazine *Times Higher Education* ranks 6 of Australia's Go8 universities among the world's 'Top 100', and another 14 Australian universities as among the world's "best universities that are 50 years old or younger".[36] That alone accounts for 20 of Australians 38 Table A universities, with other universities qualifying in the global Top 100 on a variety of other rankings as well. All in all, more than two-thirds of all Australian universities have been ranked in the global Top 100 on at least one major ranking system in the last three years. These results are inconsistent with the proposition that Australia's universities are severely underfunded.

It stands to reason that if their outcomes have been so extraordinarily good—and no other country in the world places such a large proportion of its universities on global top 100 lists—Australian universities' inputs must at least be sufficient. The most relevant questions to be answered are thus more about qualities like the trends, composition, sustainability, and fairness of funding than about the sheer quantity of funding. Such qualitative judgements require a detailed look at the sources of university funding and how they have changed over time. The most comprehensive source of revenue data for Australian universities is the annual DESE publication *Financial Reports of Higher Education Providers*. These finance reports collate revenue and expenses data for all HESA Table A higher education providers in a standard format. A summary of the revenue sources of Go8 and non-Go8 providers is presented in Table 3.

The HESA's Table A covers 38 universities plus the Batchelor Institute of Indigenous Tertiary Education. Batchelor and the six dual sector universities also have VET divisions, the revenues of which must be separated from those appertaining to their higher education divisions. Thus in constructing Table 3 (and all of the tables presented in this chapter), revenues for VET divisions have been stripped out of total revenues on an institution-by-institution basis. As a result, Table 3 encapsulates the revenues of the university higher education system, as such. For ease of presentation, Batchelor's modest higher education revenues (less than $8 million in 2019) are included in the non-Go8 and all university totals. All revenue figures reported have been adjusted to 2020 Australian dollars using the consumer price index.

Roughly half of the revenues of Australian universities are derived from Australian governments. Breaking down university finances at a very broad level, 49.2% of revenue comes directly from the Commonwealth via the HESA, with state and local government assistance pushing total government funding up

Table 3. University revenue by source, 2019 ($ 2020)

Source	Group of Eight	Percent	Non-Go8	Percent	All Universities	Percent
Australian Government Financial Assistance	$6,839,741	41.2%	$10,984,276	55.9%	$17,824,017	49.2%
==> *of which, Australian Government Grants*	*$5,172,065*	*31.1%*	*$6,835,799*	*34.8%*	*$12,007,863*	*33.1%*
State and Local Government Financial Assistance	$255,901	1.5%	$215,449	1.1%	$471,350	1.3%
Upfront Student Contributions	$173,347	1.0%	$289,607	1.5%	$462,954	1.3%
Fees and Charges	$6,009,721	36.2%	$5,715,162	29.1%	$11,724,883	32.3%
==> *of which, Fee Paying Overseas Students*	*$5,195,404*	*31.3%*	*$4,795,953*	*24.4%*	*$9,991,357*	*27.6%*
Investment Income	$1,351,130	8.1%	$853,950	4.3%	$2,205,080	6.1%
Royalties, Trademarks and Licenses	$77,866	0.5%	$58,908	0.3%	$136,774	0.4%
Consultancy and Contracts	$827,113	5.0%	$747,515	3.8%	$1,574,628	4.3%
Other Income	$1,066,604	6.4%	$783,347	4.0%	$1,849,952	5.1%
==> *of which, Donations and Bequests*	*$349,878*	*2.1%*	*$126,515*	*0.6%*	*$476,394*	*1.3%*
Share of Net Result (accounting adjustment)	$4,683	0.0%	$7,608	0.0%	$12,291	0.0%
Total Revenues from Continuing Operations	**$16,606,106**	100.0%	**$19,655,822**	100.0%	**$36,261,928**	100.0%

to 50.5%. Fee paying international students (called 'overseas' students in the DESE tables) contribute a further 27.6%. Once other miscellaneous revenues are taken into account, domestic students are left paying 6.1%, which includes course fees for non-Commonwealth-supported degrees and up front contributions that students voluntarily make so as to avoid accumulating HECS debt.

The most hotly disputed portion of the university revenue pie is the roughly 16% that the Commonwealth pays under the HESA, but not in the form of outright grants to universities. This slice includes HECS-HELP, FEE-HELP, VET FEE-HELP, VET Student Loan, and SA-HELP support. These are all forms of deferred payment that are heavily subsidised by the government. By far the largest deferred payment program is HECS-HELP, which constituted 80.8% of the category's total payments in 2019, but all four 'HELP' programs make use of the same deferred payment system. The amount to be paid is indexed to inflation, but no interest in charged, and former students only have to make payments when their incomes exceed a legislated threshold. Repayment requirements then rise with income. The whole system thus resembles a personalised graduate tax more than a loan. Nonetheless, it is widely understood as (and accounted for as) a series of loan programs.

This discrepancy lies at the heart of much of the debate over Australian university funding. Shifts over time from Commonwealth grants to HECS support can be interpreted as declines in government funding, if HECS and other HELP payments made to universities are regarded as loans taken out by students. Yet from a political economy perspective the concessional terms of the various HELP programs make them, in practice, targeted income taxes on high-income, university-educated professionals, with those who have benefitted from optional, government-subsidised higher education paying a higher effective tax rate than their peers who did not attend universities. The fundamental question isn't whether or not taxpayers should subsidise university education; it's which taxpayers: those who benefit from the degrees (i.e., the students themselves), or those who don't (i.e. everyone else).

From the university standpoint it shouldn't matter much whether Commonwealth payments are structured as grants, loans, or taxes. Nor should universities much care whether domestic students take up Commonwealth-supported places or pay full tuition for their studies. The dominant narrative on university funding thus completely misses the point. Instead of focusing on the generosity of government grants, or even on the grants-versus-loans debate, it should focus instead on the total domestic funding provided to universities for the purpose of educating Australian students. This should include funding for the teaching, scholarship, service, and engagement connected with the broad mission of educating Australian students. These are, after all, the basic activities that the Higher Education Standards Framework (2021) requires of all Australian universities.

Figure 1 charts the level of university funding in Australia that can be attributed specifically to the education of domestic Australian students. This series ('funding for domestic study') includes the DESE categories of Australian Government Financial Assistance, State and Local Government Financial Assistance, Upfront Student Contributions, and Student Fees and Charges (with the exception of Fee Paying Overseas Students). It does not include revenues from Investment Income, Royalties, Trademarks and Licenses, Consultancy and Contracts, or Other Income (like Donations and Bequests), since although these are derived largely from domestic Australian sources, their main purposes are not necessarily the education of Australian students. All figures are expressed in 2020 dollars.

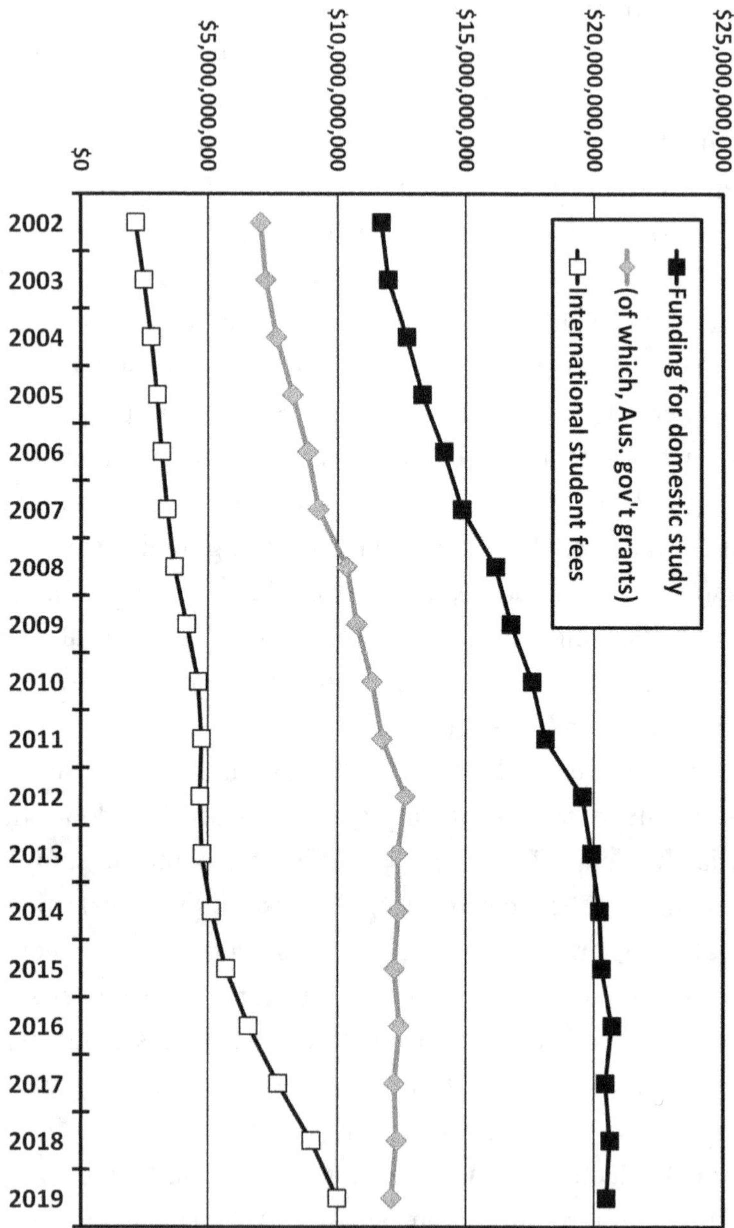

Figure 1. Real revenue by source ($ 2020)

As is clear from Figure 1, total funding for domestic study rose consistently until 2016, after which it leveled off. The grant component of this funding leveled off earlier, in 2012. In 2019, the last year before the coronavirus disruption, funding for domestic study was only 1.0% below its historical record, while Australian government grants were 4.4% off their all-time high. Thus although a narrative can be spun to suggest that Australian government grant funding has been cut substantially since 2012, the true financial situation facing universities is that total funding for domestic study has been stable at near-record levels throughout the second half of the 2010s. And if the Go8 results reported in Table 2 (compiled from individual university annual reports) turn out to be indicative of the sector as a whole, it is likely that total system-wide funding for domestic study will prove to have been at or near record levels in 2020.

Despite these relatively stable levels of domestic funding, Australian universities sought out dramatically increased levels of international student revenue after 2013. The natural inclination—encouraged by universities and their trade associations—would be to link the rapid increase in international student revenue to the slow deterioration in government grant funding that set in after 2012. But although government grant funding declined, total funding attributable to the universities' core mission of educating domestic students was actually higher at the end of the latest international student boom (2019) than it was at the beginning (2013). International student revenue constituted a rapidly rising proportion of total Australian university revenue throughout the early 2020s, tripling from 9.1% in 1999 to 27.6% in 2019, but it was always nothing more than froth on the funding cappuccino. International student income supplemented, but did not substitute for, domestic funding provided on behalf of Australian students.

Attributing revenues to students

Of course, none of this accounts for costs. Universities have both fixed costs (like campus infrastructure) and variable costs (primarily staff-related), both of which rise with the number of students being educated. Strangely, Australian universities generally seem to regard fixed costs as being borne entirely by domestic students, treating the fees paid by international students in purely marginal terms. In this self-serving model, the 100 domestic students in a hypothetical class pay for the classroom, while the additional 48 international students (and that is the average ratio) sit in the wings. Obviously, this is nonsense. Once international students cease to be valued primarily for contributing diversity and come instead to be valued primarily for contributing revenues, they must be expected to pay their fair share of a university's fixed costs. They might even be expected to pay more, since (being far from home) they are likely to use campus resources more intensively than their domestic counterparts.

Attributing both fixed and variable costs on a per-student basis across both domestic and international students dramatically simplifies the problem of determining real trends in per-student domestic funding for Australian students. If it is assumed that the average cost of educating a domestic student is equal to the average cost of educating an international student, then per-student trends in domestic versus international student revenues can be compared by simply dividing the total funding provided on behalf of each group by the total number of students (EFTSL) in each group. The EFTSL denominator for Figure 2 is taken from DESE uCube data specifically for the 39 Table A institutions. The results of these per-EFTSL calculations are charted in Figure 2.

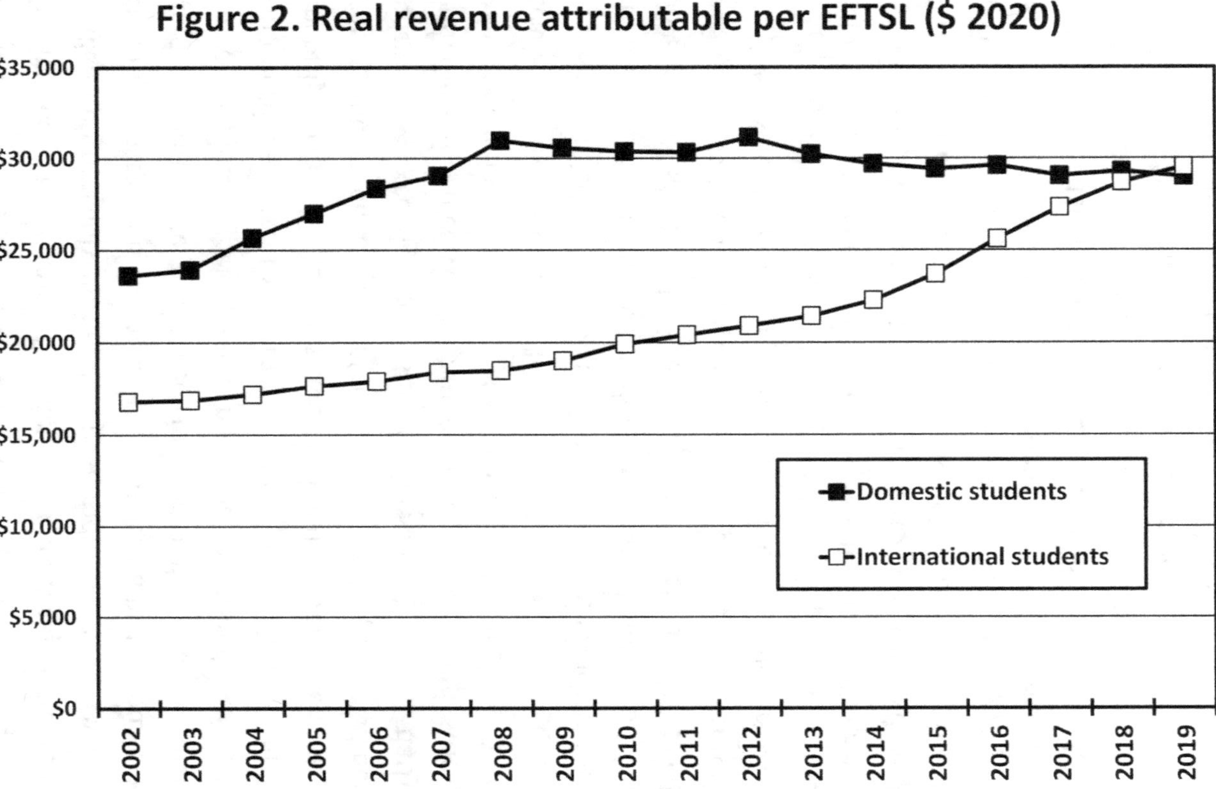

Figure 2. Real revenue attributable per EFTSL ($ 2020)
$35,000
$30,000
$25,000
$20,000
$15,000
$10,000
$5,000
$0
2002
2003
2004
2005
2006
2007
2008
2009
2010
2011
2012
2013
2014
2015
2016
2017
2018
2019
Domestic students
International students

Incredibly, per-student domestic funding for Australian students consistently exceeded per-student fee revenue paid by international students over the entire period 2002-2018. This has occurred despite the fact that international students are disproportionately enrolled in postgraduate courses (which generally charge higher fees than undergraduate courses), are disproportionately enrolled in Go8 universities (which generally charge higher fees than non-Go8 universities), and are disproportionately enrolled in capital-city universities (which generally charge higher fees than regional universities). At a system-wide level, average international revenue generated per student only exceeded domestic revenue in 2019. This flatly contradicts the received narrative promoted by universities, trade associations, and education analysts for the last two decades. It deserves a closer look.

As illustrated in Figure 2, real per-student domestic funding for Australian students rose rapidly until 2008, then stabilised between 2008 and 2012 before falling gently between 2012 and 2019. In those last seven years, the compound annual growth rate (CAGR) of per-student funding for domestic students was -0.97%, yielding a total decline of 6.9% over 7 years. This decline occurred during a period of rapidly rising domestic student numbers. Between 2012 and 2019, domestic student EFTSL at Australian universities rose 12.6%, representing a CAGR of 1.71% per year. Universities thus can rightly claim that—when evaluated on a per-student basis—they are doing more with less. The roughly 1% per year decline in per-student domestic funding is not quite the efficiency dividend of between 1.25% and 2.5% demanded by a succession of Labor and Coalition governments, but it is close.

Unfortunately, the massive expansion in international student numbers over the same period only made matters worse, not better. It imposed additional costs on the university system that had to be borne by domestic students, causing a deterioration in their university experience that far exceeded the 0.97% compound annual savings realised in domestic per-student funding. Over the entire period 2002-2019, an average of $28,680 per year was paid from all domestic sources (governments and students) in support of each domestic student place in an Australian university, while international students paid on average only $22,005 for each of their places. By paying an average of 23.3% less per place, international students were, in effect, free riding on infrastructure paid for primarily by domestic students. In other words, domestic students have been subsidising international students, not the other way around.

Viewed at a system-wide level, the funding gap between domestic and international students has closed in recent years. In 2019, international students paid an average of 1.9% more per place than the average amount paid on behalf of domestic students. This average, however, hides important disparities. Some courses attract much higher revenues per student than others, and universities differ both in their concentrations across courses and their overall tuition levels. Table 4 breaks down real student revenue per EFTSL across Go8 and non-Go8 universities. Within the Go8, international students pay 10.2% less per place than the average amount paid on behalf of domestic students. At non-Go8 universities, international students pay 0.8% less. The system-wide convergence in per-student revenue is explained by the fact that international students are concentrated in Go8 universities, where per-student revenues are higher across the board.

Looking at individual universities, the differences are even greater. Table 5 contrasts the per-student (EFTSL) revenue

Table 4. Student revenue per EFTSL, 2019 ($ 2020)

Metric	Group of Eight	Non-Go8	All Universities
All students			
Student numbers (EFTSL)	330,859	714,508	1,045,367
Real revenue per EFTSL	$40,134	$24,079	$29,160
Domestic students			
Student numbers (EFTSL)	192,850	514,152	707,002
Real revenue per EFTSL	$41,915	$24,134	$28,984
International students			
Student numbers (EFTSL)	138,008	200,352	338,360
Real revenue per EFTSL	$37,646	$23,938	$29,529
Avg. int'l student discount	**-10.2%**	**-0.8%**	**1.9%**

attributable to domestic Australian students with the tuition paid by international students for all 39 Table A institutions. Among Go8 universities (highlighted in grey), international students pay more than the funding paid on behalf of domestic students only at Sydney and Queensland. Among other universities, Macquarie, UTS, Deakin, and QUT generate the highest relative levels of international revenue per EFTSL, perhaps reflecting their prime capital city locations. At the other extreme, JCU is locationally disadvantaged for recruiting international students, while Curtin has multiple overseas campuses that may skew its data. The ANU shows the biggest gap in international versus domestic per student revenues, but this is an artefact of its extraordinarily high level of domestic funding. Its international student revenue per EFTSL is in the middle of the Go8 pack.

The effective international student discount at most Go8 universities is of particular concern, since these universities tend to charge the highest rates of tuition for international students.

Table 5. Student revenue per EFTSL, by university, 2019 ($ 2020)

University	Domestic students	International students	Difference	Percent
ACU	$20,581	$21,329	$748	3.64%
Adelaide	$38,339	$35,953	-$2,386	-6.22%
ANU	$69,563	$39,790	-$29,773	-42.80%
Batchelor	$654,396		N/A	N/A
Canberra	$24,070	$26,750	$2,680	11.14%
CDU	$25,470	$26,012	$541	2.12%
CQU	$22,252	$28,207	$5,955	26.76%
CSU	$23,862	$25,170	$1,308	5.48%
Curtin	$26,020	$16,393	-$9,627	-37.00%
Deakin	$23,481	$33,626	$10,145	43.21%
ECU	$21,020	$24,492	$3,472	16.52%
Federation	$24,881	$24,776	-$105	-0.42%
Flinders	$27,872	$27,956	$84	0.30%
Griffith	$23,409	$29,201	$5,793	24.75%
JCU	$38,219	$15,042	-$23,177	-60.64%
La Trobe	$25,613	$26,227	$613	2.40%
Macquarie	$23,646	$35,594	$11,947	50.53%
Melbourne	$42,227	$38,171	-$4,057	-9.61%
Monash	$35,425	$29,231	-$6,194	-17.48%
Murdoch	$24,362	$12,254	-$12,108	-49.70%
Newcastle	$27,571	$27,100	-$471	-1.71%
Notre Dame	$20,502	$23,100	$2,598	12.67%
Queensland	$39,762	$41,359	$1,596	4.01%
QUT	$23,352	$32,357	$9,005	38.56%
RMIT	$20,937	$19,006	-$1,931	-9.22%
SCU	$23,356	$25,333	$1,977	8.47%
Swinburne	$22,502	$19,810	-$2,692	-11.96%
Sydney	$39,274	$44,682	$5,408	13.77%
Tasmania	$32,950	$22,271	-$10,679	-32.41%
UNE	$24,613	$21,982	-$2,631	-10.69%
UNISA	$24,207	$28,534	$4,327	17.87%
UNSW	$45,080	$40,740	-$4,340	-9.63%
USC	$23,894	$25,403	$1,509	6.32%
USQ	$22,517	$25,010	$2,493	11.07%
UTS	$24,057	$34,211	$10,154	42.21%
UWA	$42,186	$34,109	-$8,077	-19.15%
Victoria	$20,671	$11,197	-$9,474	-45.83%
Wollongong	$28,813	$16,144	-$12,668	-43.97%
WSU	$20,308	$25,376	$5,067	24.95%

International student fees at a typical Go8 university can be up to double those at some non-Go8 universities. In fact, the figures reported in Table 4 show that the Go8 as a whole generates 57% more revenue per international student EFTSL than does the rest of Australia's university system. Thus it is especially surprising that the Go8, as a whole, generates substantially less international revenue per student than domestic revenue. The especially large gap at ANU points to the solution to this puzzle. Although Go8 universities generate 57% more revenue per international student than other universities, they generate 74% more revenue per domestic student than other universities. This is primarily due to the fact that the Commonwealth funds research at Go8 universities more generously than at other universities.

The key to understanding all of these figures is the attribution of Commonwealth research funding to the education of domestic students. Universities might object that research funding has nothing to do with student support, but the HESA strongly suggests otherwise: it only funds research conducted by higher education providers, not research as such. Where research funding is not intended to support to education, it can more effectively be routed through dedicated research institutions like CSIRO, or put out to tender. Research funding under the HESA exists specifically to support institutions that teach students, with the strong implication that the researchers are the people doing the teaching. Or to put it differently, it seems unlikely that the Commonwealth would fund research at a university that was dedicated to educating only international students. If international students are not paying enough to support the research of the professors who teach them, they are not subsidising the system, but being subsidised by it.

The cost of education

If Australian universities did not, on balance, benefit from expanding international student numbers, then why did they do it? The answer is probably to be found in an accounting fallacy that runs deep in government and university thinking about the workings of universities. It is the portrayal of a university as an organisation that offers educational services on a marginal basis, instead of as an organisation that is primarily dedicated to education. The 2019 Deloitte Access Economics report that has been so influential in informing government policy is steeped in this misunderstanding of university operations. It presents a bottom-up costing of university courses that attributes the marginal costs of education to student enrolments. Incredibly, this results in a finding that Australian universities devote on average only 52% of their resources to 'teaching and scholarship'.[37] Their estimate for Go8 universities is just 39%. That is, frankly, ridiculous.

If universities are spending only 52% of their money on teaching and scholarship, what are they doing with the other 48%? Deloitte seems to consider big-ticket institutional 'research' that falls outside of the ordinary knowledge-production activities of academic teaching staff to be a separate activity from 'scholarship', but the proportion of research-only academics in Australian universities is relatively small. They can't possibly make up more than a few percentage points of the total costs of running the university system. Deloitte also treats community service activities as outside its remit, but again this is a minor issue. Without telling us where the other 48% is going, Deloitte's bottom-up 52% figure is simply not credible. Are student services included in 'teaching and scholarship'? Is running the university's communications infrastructure? Filling the campus pool? Washing the office windows? What about mowing the lawn?

If some phantom non-teaching entity washes the windows and mows the lawn, leaving teaching to be conducted in classrooms that mysteriously clean themselves, then Deloitte's figure of $18,500 per EFTSL (2018 dollars) makes sense. But given that the main business activity of a university is teaching and scholarship, the general overhead costs of a university must be charged against teaching and scholarship. Deloitte seems to have costed teaching and scholarship from the bottom up without including a charge for general university overhead. The Commonwealth should not have accepted this at face value. It should either have demanded a refund from the universities—or from Deloitte.

The classrooms, the offices, even the lawns and tennis courts of universities exist to deliver 'teaching and scholarship' because the university as an organisation exists to deliver teaching and scholarship. These costs are part and parcel of the business of educating students. By viewing campus overhead as an infinitely flexible fixed cost to be borne by domestic students alone (or, in Deloitte's model, by no one), university administrators have tricked themselves, the government, and the public into believing that international students generate extraordinary surpluses.[38] At the margin, they do. But when one-third of the university system's 'teaching and scholarship' is devoted to educating international students, they must be considered part of the core 'customer' base of the organisation.

When Australia's current university landscape took shape some three decades ago, the country enrolled relatively few international students, and nearly all of them were on scholarships. It has been estimated that there were only 1000 fee-paying international students in Australia in 1987.[39] The basic vocabulary of today's Commonwealth funding system was put in place in this era, and thus it should come as no surprise that the onshore education of international students was treated as a residual, and implicitly as a charity gesture. At the time, most of Australia's policy attention with regard to international education focused on offshore programs, not onshore ones.[40] Most of these overseas campuses in Southeast Asia, which once formed the great hope of Australian universities for international expansion, have now closed. Forced to charge the full costs of their operations against the international student revenues they generated, they simply couldn't pay the bills.

It turned out that what Asian students wanted wasn't so much an Australian degree as an Australian education, experienced in Australia. But if these students are going to study onshore, in Australia, sharing facilities with Australian domestic students, they cannot be accounted for as a purely marginal revenue source. They are no more marginal than Australian students are. Just as international students taught offshore must bear the full costs of running Australian offshore campuses, international students taught onshore must bear (pro rata) the full costs of running Australian onshore campuses. By that simple, straightforward logic, onshore international students have long been 'unprofitable' for most Australian universities, and for the Australian university system as a whole. Accounted for on a pro rata basis, they have not paid their fair share.

The myth that international students have long subsidised domestic ones is based on a deep-seated misunderstanding of university political economy. The fundamental mistake made by participants in the university funding debate has been to value international students in purely marginal terms, as if they could be 'squeezed into' existing infrastructure without contributing to universities' ongoing fixed costs. In other words, it has been assumed that Australian universities as institutions should be funded by the Commonwealth, with only the marginal costs of teaching international students charged against their tuition payments. That model may have been a reasonable approximation of reality thirty years ago, when international student numbers were relatively trivial. It has clearly outlived its usefulness at a time when international students occupy nearly one-third of all seats in Australian university classrooms.

* * *

Are Australia's universities 'underfunded'? No, they are not. Adequate funding is a slippery concept, but Commonwealth funding for Australia's universities is medium-high by international standards and has been relatively stable since 2012. In per-EFTSL terms, domestic Australian payments from all sources made to universities on behalf of domestic students fell 6.9% between 2012 and 2019, but in light of the 12.6% increase in domestic student EFTSL, this can probably be subsumed within economies of scale. That is to say, there was less funding per student because there were more students sharing the same basic campus resources. The domestic funding decline between 2012 and 2019 represents a gently declining CAGR, or 'efficiency dividend', of 1% annually. Even that figure overstates the true decline in domestic funding experienced by individual institutions, since it is skewed by a decline in the proportion of domestic students being taught by high-revenue Go8 universities.

Domestic enrolments rose at both Go8 and non-Go8 universities between 2012 and 2019, but they rose faster outside the Go8, which is to say: at universities that attract relatively lower levels of funding per student. Within each subset of universities, domestic funding per domestic EFTSL fell less than 1% per year, substantially less in the case of Go8 universities.

Table 6. Growth in students and revenue (CAGR 2012-2019)

Metric	Group of Eight	Non-Go8	All Universities
All students			
Student numbers (EFTSL)	3.66%	2.65%	2.96%
Real revenue per EFTSL	-2.76%	-1.44%	-1.90%
Domestic students			
Student numbers (EFTSL)	0.53%	2.19%	1.71%
Real revenue per EFTSL	-0.65%	-0.85%	-0.97%
International students			
Student numbers (EFTSL)	9.88%	3.94%	6.05%
Real revenue per EFTSL	2.06%	3.75%	3.49%

In about one-third of universities, domestic funding for domestic students actually grew. These trends are summarised in Table 6. Ironically, revenue generated per EFTSL for all students fell much faster than domestic revenue generated per domestic student because, over most of the period, international student revenue per EFTSL was lower than domestic student revenue per EFTSL (as illustrated in Figure 2). Thus as universities expanded relentlessly into overseas markets, they were steadily eroding their average revenues generated per EFTSL.

It has repeatedly been argued that the end of the demand-driven model in 2018 forced universities to turn overseas to find students to fill their classrooms, but this is not supported by the data. The demand-driven model was an approach to university financing in which universities were allowed to enrol unlimited numbers of domestic students into Commonwealth-supported places. It was introduced in 2010 and ended abruptly—with only a few weeks' notice—at the end of 2017. The first two years were transition years. In the early years of the demand-driven era, Commonwealth grants and HELP support rose with the number of domestic students. After

2012, grant funding flattened, but HELP support continued to track rising student numbers. But in 2017, the final year of the demand-driven model, domestic EFTSL at Australian universities grew by just 0.7%.

International EFTSL shot up by 10.2%.

Having tapped out the domestic market and its uncapped supply of generously-funded, government-subsidised domestic students, in 2017 the universities turned to low-margin international students instead. They did this while the demand-driven model was still in place, with no foreknowledge during the 2016 international recruiting season that the demand-driven model would end one year hence. The obvious interpretation is that the universities turned overseas simply to maintain their accustomed rates of enrolment growth. Between 2001 and 2019, Australian universities increased their total EFTSL enrolments at a relatively constant CAGR of 3.3%. Annual enrolment growth was somewhat volatile in the first decade after the turn of the century, but throughout the 2010s it remained steady at between 2.0% and 3.5%. Having planned for endless growth, they may simply have used international recruitment to fill already-budgeted places.

The CAGR of the Australian university system's total EFTSL was 3.4% in the 8 years prior to the demand-driven era, 3.2% during the 8 years of the demand-driven era, and 2.9% in the two years after the end of the demand-driven era. This is the record of an industry reaching saturation, first in its home market, then in its second market (China), then going farther and farther afield in a futile search for everlasting growth. As the industry matured, marginal revenues, quite naturally, declined toward marginal costs—or at least, the marginal costs of teaching additional students within current campus settings. It's Microeconomics 101, not a government conspiracy to "wage war on our universities".[41] No business grows forever. It's not clear that universities should grow at all.

In 2018, ANU announced that it would halt enrolment growth, right-sizing the university at around 20,000 full-time students.[42] Its vice chancellor has since lamented that "missing a year's growth of student revenue meant the pandemic has hit us harder than anyone in the sector".[43] He didn't mention that the ANU lost twice as much in investment revenue as in international student fees, or that it suffered a proportional decline in international student fee revenue that was five times that of the rest of the Go8. If the ANU was thrown into "chaos from the pandemic-driven shock to our business model", it seems to have been the result of either uniquely poor financial management or uniquely bad luck.

Either way, the university's previous decision to draw the line at 20,000 students likely saved ANU from more severe losses. The university is correct to argue that it was in robust financial health before the pandemic. But the further the university went down the international student recruitment path, the more that health would have deteriorated. Instead of taking away the headline message not to limit their growth like ANU did, other universities should learn the deeper lesson that ANU rightsized at 20,000 students. Most of Australia's universities would be more financially sustainable had they capped international enrolments at 2010 levels and avoided the 2014-2019 international student binge. They would be smaller, healthier, more stable institutions.

If one accepts the general principle that university enrolment growth must end eventually, the only question is when. Australia's public universities are already very large by international standards, with four (Monash, Melbourne, Sydney, and RMIT) that would rank among the 10 largest public universities in all of North America. And with roughly one international student for every two domestic students, Australia already has proportionally the largest international student population in the world (and absolutely the second, trailing only the United States). If it really is true that Australia's universities are chronically starved of funding, it may be because they keep seeking low-margin, high-volatility international growth. A saner future would see them consolidate around their high-margin, low-volatility domestic student base.

CHAPTER 3

How many international students are too many?

We live in a global age, and everyone agrees that universities should leaven their student bodies with a diverse mix of students from around the world. Hosting international students is a way for universities to expose their domestic students to international experiences before they ever leave home. It also helps domestic students learn how to navigate the complexities of working alongside and befriending people from different countries and cultures. Universities often brag on their websites about having "alumni in more than 170 countries" (Sydney), "students from 150+ countries" (Melbourne), or students "from 142 countries" (Queensland). Meanwhile governments see international education as a tool of public diplomacy. The Commonwealth's New Colombo Plan, initiated in 2014, brings dozens of talented Asian students to Australia every year. It's a drop in the ocean, but a symbolic one all the same.

Some university ranking systems even give credit for the proportion of students who come from overseas. But, as always, it is possible to have too much of a good thing. In 2002, the Australian university system as a whole generated 20.5% of its EFTSL from international students, more than the single most internationalised public university in the United States at the time: the Australian average was greater than the American maximum. By 2019, international students accounted for 32.4% of Australian system-wide EFTSL, and 25 out of Australia's 37 public universities were more internationalised than any public university in the entire United States. In fact, Australia enrols proportionally more international students than any other major country in the world—by far.[44]

In some courses, the numbers of international students hosted by Australian universities have reached such epic proportions that English is no longer the most widely-spoken native language in the classroom. In postgraduate coursework degrees in business at Sydney, Melbourne, and Queensland, more than 80% of the students are international.[45] They don't advertise these figures on their websites; in fact, they are only available at all due to the programs' accreditation with the Association to Advance Collegiate Schools of Business (AACSB), a US-based accreditation body. Chinese postgraduate students at Australian business schools routinely complain that they have few opportunities to practice English.[46] The concentration of Chinese and other international students in most other programs is not that extreme, but it is still extraordinary by international standards. Seven of the 8 largest Chinese universities outside China are in Australia.[47]

If Australian universities are already among the most international in the world, and have been since the turn of the millennium, why are so many of them so eager to continue expanding international enrolments? It's certainly not for the educational benefits of promoting a diverse campus community; that goal has long since been met. The pundits (and often the universities themselves) say that it's due to government funding cuts. But it has already been shown that government grants, though no longer growing at 6% per year (as they did between 2002 and 2012), have been relatively stable in recent years, while total domestic funding per domestic EFTSL has been falling at less than 1% per year. These are hardly catastrophic numbers, especially when seen in light of consistently stable or rising domestic enrolments.

Yet Australian universities turned aggressively to international student markets to maintain revenue growth, not once, but several times: in the early 2000s, in the wake of the Global Financial Crisis, and most recently from 2014-2019. These periods do not correspond so much to the ups and downs of domestic funding as they do to the ups and downs of the Australian dollar. In the early 2000s, the Australian dollar fell to an all-time low of less than 50 US cents, making Australian tuition very cheap for international students. During the Global Financial Crisis, the Australian dollar fell in just a few months from 95 cents to 65 cents, again lowering the international cost of an Australian education. And after trading above parity with the US dollar throughout much of 2011-2013, the Australia dollar fell again for a final time in 2014. These trends are depicted in Figure 3, which charts the Australian dollar exchange rate against international student enrolments.

The correspondence is near-perfect: statistically speaking, the correlation is $r = -0.864$. This strongly suggests that changes in international student enrolment over the last two decades have been driven entirely by fluctuating exchange rates. In fact, the number of outbound Chinese tertiary students going to all countries was not at all cyclical, but continually increased between 1998 and 2018, according to United Nations data (data are not yet available for 2019 and 2020). Modest 2012 declines in outbound numbers from India and Nepal (Australia's second and third largest sources of international students) were swamped by the increase in Chinese numbers that year. For two decades, the international student market was consistently growing, but in

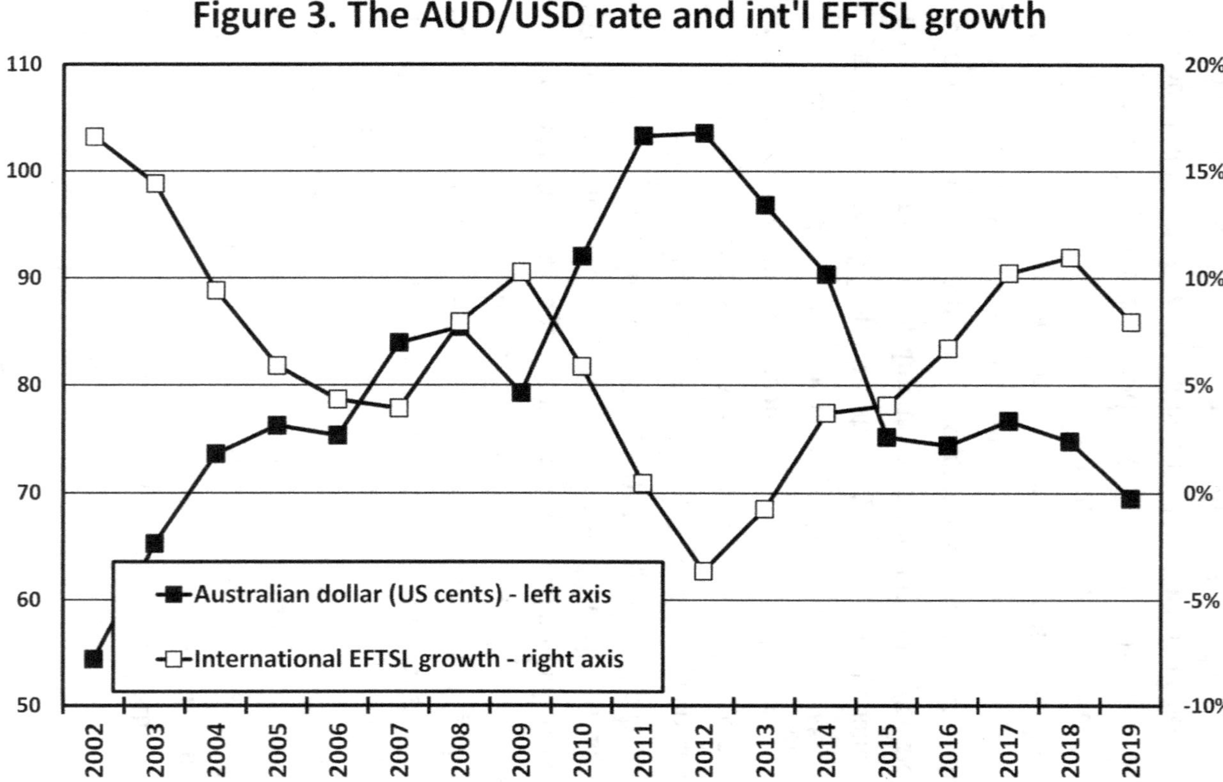
Figure 3. The AUD/USD rate and int'l EFTSL growth
Australian dollar (US cents) - left axis
International EFTSL growth - right axis
110
100
90
80
70
60
50
20%
15%
10%
5%
0%
-5%
-10%
2002
2003
2004
2005
2006
2007
2008
2009
2010
2011
2012
2013
2014
2015
2016
2017
2018
2019

certain years students seemingly avoided Australia—not because Commonwealth support for universities was sufficiently generous in those years, but because a strong Australian dollar drove up the international prices of Australian degrees.

The received narrative that Australian universities turned to the international market to make up for domestic funding shortfalls simply is not reflected in the data. International student commencements in Australia clearly responded to market pressures, not university needs. And Australian universities have increasingly pursued international students using commercial methods, opening promotional offices overseas (especially China), producing marketing materials in multiple languages (especially Chinese), and expanding their use of commission-based recruitment agents (especially in China). Universities and their trade associations also increasingly use the language of business in justifying their push overseas, constantly spruiking their success as services exporters. With the coming of the coronavirus crisis, several universities even offered discounts to international students who were unable to travel to Australia.[48]

Price sensitivity, agency fees, export success—these are the language of business, not of public service. Public economics does a poor job of explaining the Australian university sector's push into international student markets. In the aggressive pursuit of ever more international students, Australian universities have been behaving neither as government entities nor as not-for-profit organisations. They have been behaving as for-profit businesses. Of course, public universities are not businesses, and as not-for-profit organisations they cannot turn a profit. But their behaviour in pursuing international students more closely corresponds to the expectations of business economics than to those of public economics. Australia's one for-profit university, Torrens, was 61% international by EFTSL in 2019 (the most recent year for which data are available). Many of the country's public universities seem to harbour ambitions to match it.

Bowen's Law and international students

The true reason for Australian universities' aggressive pursuit of international students is not to be found in their domestic funding arrangements. According to the theory of public economics, taxpayer-supported public service organisations are expected to do their best to fulfil their missions with whatever resources are put at their disposal for the purpose: that is, to achieve the best possible outcomes for a given level of inputs. For example, the Australian Defence Force is expected to "defend Australia and its national interests in order to advance Australia's security and prosperity".[49] It has a duty to responsibly spend the funds put at its disposal for that purpose, but it does not seek extra revenue if it feels that its funding is inadequate. It does the best job it can with the resources it has been given. The same is true for public sector organisations that generate customer revenue to supplement their government grants. A museum may charge admission fees, but its mission is to responsibly discharge its duties as a museum while generating sufficient revenue to ensure its continued existence. It is not expected to maximise admission revenue or turn a 'profit'.

Public universities are (or should be) no different. Their mission is primarily the education of domestic students, and their resources consist primarily of government grants, supplemented by student fees. Universities also conduct research in support of their educational missions, on the theory (written into the Higher Education Standards Framework) that "academic and teaching staff are active in scholarship that informs their teaching". Thus when universities find that the average per-student revenues at their disposal exceed their average per-student costs, they should in theory either return the excess to the taxpayers or use their surpluses to improve the education of their students. The first option is perhaps unthinkable, but the second at least should occur to the mind of the diligent vice chancellor. This principle is known as 'Bowen's Law', which has been paraphrased as "universities raise all the money they can, and spend all the money they raise".[50]

This 'revenue theory of cost' is not merely a clever maxim, but a serious theory of university economics.[51] It posits that "nonprofits exist to provide as much service as possible, and internal constituents can always find ways to use financial resources".[52] This is viewed as a major problem in the United States, where most university revenues derive from student fees. There, universities are able to extract ever-higher fees from students because of their monopoly over the granting of degrees, which are widely viewed as indispensable entry tickets into white-collar professions. In theory, this should not be a problem in Australia, since the Commonwealth exercises effective control over the pricing of most domestic undergraduate degrees (and many postgraduate ones).

If Australian universities behaved as typical not-for-profit organisations in accordance with Bowen's Law, they would not have turned to international student recruitment to increase revenue. Even if their revenues fell short of their ambitions, they would have adjusted the scale of their ambitions to match the resources at their disposal. Analysed from a public economics perspective, there is no such thing as an underfunded university. A poorly-funded university can have 1000-student classes with no tutorials, as is the case in many large US state universities. A richly-funded university like Oxford or Cambridge can have 20-student classes with one-on-one tutorials. A poorly-funded university can have its classes taught by obscure scholars with few publications. A richly-funded university can have its classes taught by Nobel laureates. Neither ever experiences a funding shortfall, since it would be expected to match its educational experiences to its funding level.

Thus in a highly-centralised system like Australia's, where the government controls the funding of university study, Bowen's Law in effect lets the government determine the overall system-wide quality of education. The specific quality of education at each institution might be further shaped by the skill of its managers and the efficiency of its bureaucracy. Other factors might also shape outcomes, like inherited traditions of scholarship or the desirability of a capital city location. But, broadly speaking, they will spend what the government gives them (or allows them to get). Most public universities in countries where university funding is largely in the hands of the government are sleepy public service entities that behave in accordance with these widely accepted principles of not-for-profit management.

Not Australia's. For good or for bad, Australia's universities do not behave as public economics would predict. In public economics, the classic challenge of government funding is the 'principal/agent problem': the taxpayers (the principals) are liable to be fleeced by the universities (their agents) because universities are always incentivised to deliver more educational services than necessary, at ever-rising costs to taxpayers. That was the fundamental problem of Australia's demand-driven model. From 2010 to 2017, universities were incentivised to admit as many domestic students as possible, since Commonwealth grant funding was not limited by budget constraints, but only by the number of students the universities could enrol. Romantic notions of unlimited education notwithstanding, the demand-driven model was a principal/agent problem straight out of the public economics textbooks.

But the principal/agent problem does not apply to Australian universities' forays into the international student market. International students come to Australia voluntarily, and as Figure 3 demonstrates, they are highly price-sensitive. Unlike domestic students, they are inherently mobile customers empowered with extensive consumer choice. In such a situation, the rational response of a for-profit university would be to admit international students up until the point where the marginal cost of providing an additional student place equals the marginal per-student revenue (tuition fees) that international students are willing to pay. In this for-profit model, the last few international students admitted are only 'marginally profitable' for the university, but for-profit organisations are incentivised to squeeze every last penny of profit out of the market.

The rational response of a public sector university should be somewhat different. Australia's Table A universities are funded to educate domestic students on the basis of average costs: the Commonwealth estimates the average cost of funding a student place in a particular course, and provides funding (or causes students to provide funding) on that basis. Combining Bowen's Law with the theory that spending determines quality, the quality of education in these courses is determined by the average revenue per student set by the government. That places a moral duty on universities to sell places to international students at no less than the average cost paid on behalf of domestic students. Even better, if the average tuition fees paid by international students exceed the average per-student revenues paid on behalf of domestic students, educational quality will improve.

Most Australian universities, however, seem to embrace the marginal-revenue model of international student recruitment that is characteristic of for-profit firms. They seem to continue recruiting internationally as long as the tuition fees paid by international students exceed the marginal costs of providing additional student places. This for-profit behaviour results in stratospherically high international student enrolments compared to those found at public universities in other countries. It also inevitably brings down the average quality of the education provided to domestic students, since all students in a classroom receive the same education. When Australian students are funded on an average-cost basis while international students are admitted on a marginal-revenue basis, the net result is that international students are effectively subsidised by domestic ones. It's no wonder so many international students want to study in Australia.

The pervasive legend that 'international students are highly profitable' really is true—or would be, if public universities were for-profit organisations. Australia's public universities are funded as not-for-profit organisations on the domestic side (average revenues equal average costs) but sell additional student places on the international side (marginal revenues equal marginal costs). At the margin, in this model the final international student admitted generates lower revenue at higher cost than the average domestic student, bringing down the average per-student educational expenditure of the university, and thus reducing the overall quality of education. Recourse to the international market in effect allows universities to convert their fixed per-student public funding into free cash flow by monetising reductions in educational quality. This free cash flow can then be spent at the vice chancellor's discretion. Highly profitable indeed.

International students by the numbers

Most Australians are aware that the country hosts a large number of international students. They may not be aware just how many. Table 7 reports numbers of international tertiary students hosted

Table 7. Top 10 destination countries for international students (2018)

Country	Number of Int'l students	Percent of world total	Int'l students per 1000 pop.	Ratio of inbound to outbound
United States	987,314	17.7%	3.0	11.7
United Kingdom	452,079	8.1%	6.7	11.6
Australia	444,514	8.0%	17.9	33.4
Germany	311,738	5.6%	3.8	2.5
Russia	262,416	4.7%	1.8	N/A
France	229,623	4.1%	3.5	2.3
Canada	224,548	4.0%	6.1	4.6
Japan	182,748	3.3%	1.4	5.7
China	178,271	3.2%	0.1	1.0
Turkey	125,138	2.2%	1.5	2.6
World	**5,571,402**	**100.0%**	**0.7**	**N/A**

by the top 10 destination countries for 2018 (the most recent year for which data are available) using data from the United Nations. Note that the figures reported in Table 7 are student counts, not EFTSLs. Australia had the third largest international student population in the world in 2018, and actually overtook the UK in 2019 to enter second place, according to data from national sources. That's quite impressive for a country of just 25 million people. Leaving aside micro-states like Luxembourg and San Marino, Australia has by far the highest concentration of international students as a proportion of its population, exceeding 20 international students per 1000 population in 2019. This is internationally unparalleled.

What's more, Australia's international student population is actually even higher than the figures reported in Table 7 suggest. In Australia, New Zealand citizens do not count as 'international' students. Nor do permanent residents of Australia and their children. Since Australia has among the highest non-citizen resident populations among major countries (trailing only Switzerland), its concentration of non-citizen domestic students would be correspondingly higher than in other countries. Moreover, Australia's international students tend to be much more 'foreign' than those in other countries. In the United Kingdom, roughly 30% of international students come from European Union countries. In Germany and France the situation is similar. Many of Russia's international students come from former Soviet republics. Australia's, by contrast, tend to come from culturally dissimilar countries in East, South, and Southeast Asia.

Australia's concentration of international students per capita is nearly three times that of the UK and six times that of the US. Australia also has by far the most unbalanced flow of international students in the world. In 2018, the number of international students in Australia was more than 33 times the number of Australian students who went abroad. That's nearly triple the ratio in the US and UK, and more than triple New Zealand's ratio of 10.5. Other countries that are major hosts of international students are at the same time major donors of international students to other countries. Only in Australia is the flow so extreme—and at the same time so lopsided.

It is not clear from the UN documentation exactly what kinds of students are included in these figures; for example, the UN reported that there were 444,514 international tertiary students in Australia in 2018, while DESE reported 480,110 (a figure that rose to 523,748 in 2019). Nonetheless, the data are intended by the UN to be broadly comparable across countries. And they show that Australia falls far outside the parameters set by other countries. The only country that even comes close to Australia in international students per 1000 population is New Zealand, and in 2018 New Zealand's ratio was 11.1, compared to Australia's 17.9. Assuming that most of Australia's international students fall between the ages of 18 and 30, roughly 20% of the entire population of the country in that age range consists of international students. No other major country in the world comes close.

In 2001, Australia's ratio of 8.1 international higher education students per 1000 population (approximated using DESE data) was already the highest in the world—and higher than that of any major host country today. The growth in Australia's international student numbers since then has been staggering. Zeroing in on universities, in 2001 there were 157,102 international students at Australia's Table A universities, generating an EFTSL of 109,784 (according to DESE data). By 2019, this had risen to 442,701 students generating an EFTSL of 338,363. That represents a 182% growth in students numbers, generating a 208% growth in EFTSL. As depicted in Figure 4, the growth has been stronger at Go8 universities (304%) than at non-Go8 universities (165%), but nonetheless extraordinary at both. More than 40% of all of Australia's international student EFTSL is now generated within the Go8, up from an average of around 30% over the period 2001-2010.

International student EFTSL doubled at Go8 universities in the first decade of the twenty-first century, then doubled again in the second decade. It now exceeds 40% of the total EFTSL generated by Go8 universities—or at least, it did before the pandemic. Table 8 reports international EFTSL proportions and growth rates for all 39 Table A institutions, highlighting the Go8 universities. Extreme levels of international EFTSL are now the rule at all Go8 universities except UWA, although even UWA has a higher concentration of international students than any public university in the entire United States. Some non-Go8 universities have matched and even exceeded Go8 levels of international EFTSL concentration: Federation, RMIT, Victoria, and Wollongong all exceed the Go8 average, and another 13 have higher international student concentrations than UWA.

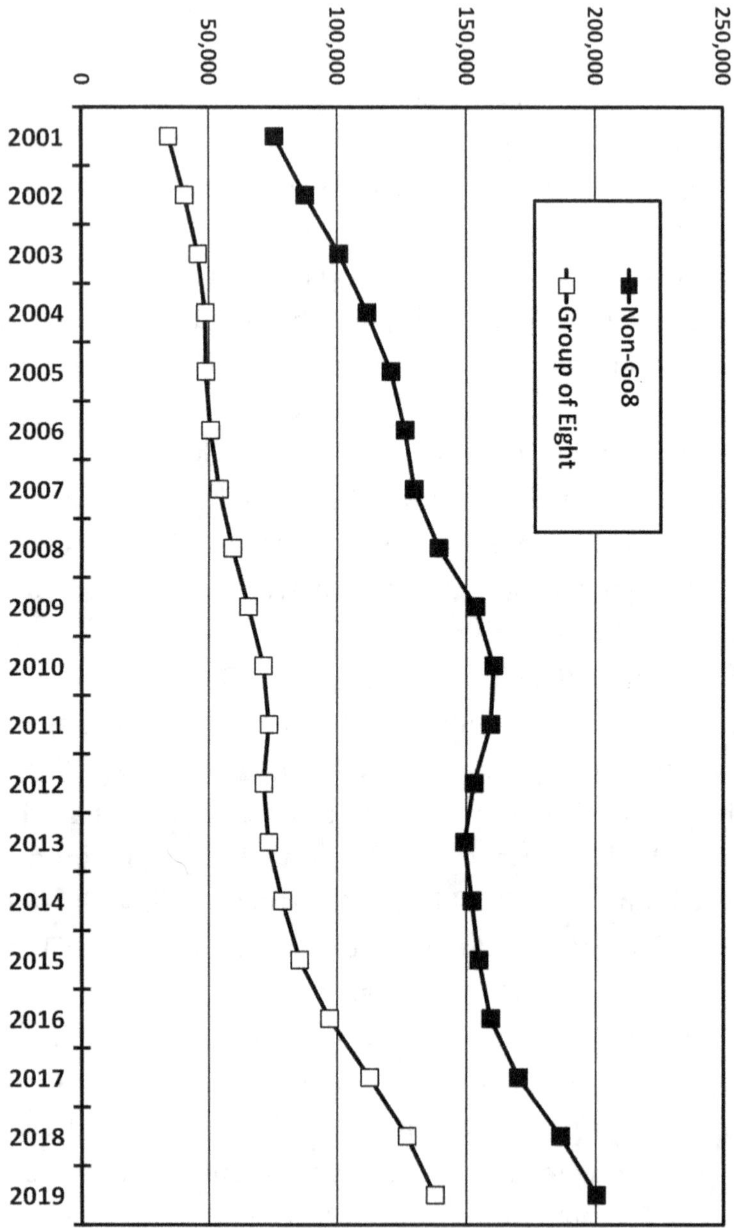

Figure 4. Int'l EFTSLs at Australian universities

Table 8. Growth in international student EFTSL, 2001-2019

University	2001 percent International	2019 percent International	2001-2019 Int'l EFTSL growth
ACU	5.4%	14.2%	766.5%
Adelaide	12.6%	32.2%	375.4%
ANU	16.7%	42.1%	490.4%
Batchelor	0.0%	0.0%	N/A
Canberra	16.4%	22.2%	117.3%
CDU	7.2%	21.0%	570.8%
CQU	43.6%	37.2%	6.2%
CSU	21.9%	26.6%	47.1%
Curtin	32.4%	29.4%	49.1%
Deakin	11.6%	28.5%	459.7%
ECU	14.4%	24.4%	129.9%
Federation	19.5%	55.3%	752.5%
Flinders	10.5%	20.4%	266.6%
Griffith	14.4%	18.3%	118.3%
JCU	9.3%	36.5%	546.5%
La Trobe	11.9%	26.6%	267.9%
Macquarie	19.8%	27.8%	177.0%
Melbourne	18.4%	43.8%	332.1%
Monash	26.2%	49.4%	276.6%
Murdoch	23.6%	39.7%	223.8%
Newcastle	9.1%	17.8%	222.0%
Notre Dame	0.0%	2.0%	N/A
Queensland	13.1%	37.9%	360.8%
QUT	13.1%	19.8%	131.4%
RMIT	34.9%	46.5%	177.2%
SCU	12.1%	32.0%	383.8%
Swinburne	22.9%	31.1%	274.3%
Sydney	13.7%	44.4%	450.4%
Tasmania	9.5%	29.2%	554.6%
UNE	5.6%	9.8%	161.4%
UNISA	26.4%	21.3%	-5.2%
UNSW	24.6%	39.7%	179.3%
USC	5.8%	21.3%	1750.4%
USQ	21.2%	13.8%	-16.2%
UTS	16.5%	33.2%	268.1%
UWA	14.0%	23.8%	149.2%
Victoria	18.3%	43.6%	274.1%
Wollongong	26.7%	43.4%	254.5%
WSU	16.5%	17.7%	55.0%

Nearly all Australian universities enrol international students (and particularly Chinese students) well in excess of accepted practices in most other countries. They are absolutely exceptional by European Union and North American standards. Even in Canada, where universities enrol more international students than in the US, McGill University is the most internationalised public university at almost 31%, followed by the University of British Columbia (roughly 27%), the University of Windsor (23%), the University of Toronto (21%), and Simon Fraser University (17%). In New Zealand, the University of Auckland is by far the most internationalised public university in the country, at 25% international. These figures are taken from the respective universities' own publications. System-wide concentrations of international students are much lower.

Perhaps the closest comparison to the Australian system is that of the United Kingdom, which hit an all-time high of 22.0% international by headcount in 2019 (including 5.8% from the European Union and 16.2% non-EU).[53] Although that placed the UK still far behind Australia's 2019 international student headcount concentration of 32.5% (for all higher education providers), several highly internationalised British universities rival or even surpass Australian ones. The London School of Economics is by far in the lead, at roughly two-thirds international. Unsurprisingly, other London institutions are also high in the UK international student league tables. Imperial College London and University of the Arts London are tied at 54% international, University College London is 49% international, and King's College London is 41% international. Among comprehensive public universities, Edinburgh is 41% international, Manchester is 38%, and Sheffield is 37%. Oxford and Cambridge are each roughly one-third international, again with large proportions of European Union students. These figures are taken from the Complete University Guide.

There are several reasons not to be reassured by the UK experience. First, the treatment of European Union students as non-UK contrasts with the Australian inclusion of New Zealand students in domestic statistics. Moreover the large numbers of American, Irish, Australian, and even northern European students at UK universities do not face significant language-based educational challenges. They are also less likely to experience financial stress than Australia's students, who hail mainly from much poorer countries. And it is quite natural that the United Kingdom, which lies just across a narrow channel from the rest of Europe, should attract many European students. It is perhaps equally natural that a former colonial power should continue to attract many students from the former outposts of empire.

Most importantly, however, it is entirely possible that the UK is suffering from the same problem as Australia: the underpricing of international places to generate free cash flow by spreading each university's fixed costs over a larger student base, thereby monetising reductions in educational quality. Due to a lack of EFTSL-level data for the UK, it has proven impossible to exactly replicate for the UK the comparison of per-student revenues generated by domestic versus international students. A best-effort analysis of 2019-2020 data from the Higher Education Statistics Agency suggests that total payments made on behalf of domestic and international students is roughly equal in the UK at just over £15,000 ($28,000) per EFTSL across all UK higher education providers. That is very slightly less than the 2019 average per-EFTSL international student revenue for Australia, indicating convergence across the two countries.

Time series data are not readily available for the UK, and the UK's concentration of international students in high-cost London must severely skew its data. The UK's changing relationship with the European Union also complicates its higher education finance statistics. But it is provocative that Australia and the UK—the world's two most aggressive recruiters of international students—have converged on international tuition fees that are roughly one-third less than those that prevail in Canada and the United States. On top of this, most Australian and UK undergraduate degrees take three years to complete, compared to four years in North America. Thus the total cost to an international undergraduate student of pursuing a bachelor degree in Australia or the UK is likely to be around half that in North America. That is a very attractive value proposition—for the international student. It's not clear that it is good for universities, or for the domestic students they are chartered to serve.

Market concentration: China, India, and Nepal

Whether or not Australian universities decide to resume the extraordinary international student growth of the last two decades after the pandemic pause, it is likely to prove difficult for them to do so. China is, of course, the largest source of international students for Australia (and for the world). Even before the coronavirus pause, many analysts believed that China's outbound international student market had fully matured and was unlikely to grow much in the future.[54] Since then, the pandemic has given the Chinese government an ideal opportunity to limit future student outflows. China has in recent years become much more repressive, and there are strong incentives for its government to use its almost-unlimited powers to prevent students from going abroad in the future. These include the need to preserve foreign currency reserves and anticipated future enrolment declines at its own domestic universities—to say nothing of political and foreign policy considerations.[55]

Demographics also weigh heavily against continued outbound Chinese student growth. The children of China's late-1980s baby boomlet are now between 29 and 37 years old, and having long since aged out of the undergraduate recruitment range, they are now aging out of the postgraduate range. Today's school leaver cohorts in China are nearly 40% off the peak reached in 2004. Thus it should come as no surprise that whereas the bulk of Australia's international students in the early 2000s were undergraduates, today postgraduates make up nearly half of the international student population. The postgraduate proportion from China is presumably even higher, but level of study data are only available from Austrade via a paid subscription from an organisation "with a demonstrated commitment to the best interests of the Australian education sector".[56] Individual researchers are not able to access these data.

Annual undergraduate enrolment growth at China's own universities slowed from the double digits in the early 2000s to less than 4% in the 2010s to less than 3% in recent years, according to data from China's National Bureau of Statistics. Irregularities and discontinuities in China's statistical reporting can make it difficult to establish the exact details of China's domestic higher education market, but the trend toward slower growth is clear. For non-Chinese universities that seek to educate Chinese students, much will also depend on the future growth of China's economy, which is a profound unknown. China is also in the midst of a major crackdown on foreign ideas and ideologies that has not yet (but may soon) be extended to study abroad. Whether Chinese outbound student numbers grow, stabilise, or shrink, they certainly will not return to the double-digit annual growth rates of the early 2000s.

British vice chancellors might be forgiven for believing otherwise. Annual Chinese student commencements in the UK quadrupled between 2007 and 2019.[57] Brexit, although near-universally condemned by British university vice chancellors in their public statements, has now relieved them of the requirement to admit European Union students on the same terms as UK ones. They seem to be chomping at the bit to expand Chinese enrolments. In light of China's aggressive stance toward Australia since 2019 and Australia's continuing coronavirus travel restrictions, any future growth in outbound Chinese student numbers will likely flow toward the UK rather than to Australia. Australian universities, in any case, face strong pressure from national and state auditors to 'diversify' their international student intakes away from China.

In 2020, nearly two-thirds of Australia's international students were drawn from just three countries: China (38.4%), India (18.9%), and Nepal (8.1%). The trajectories over time in enrolments from these three countries, plus a tracking line for all other countries, are plotted in Figure 5. The underlying data for Figure 5 are taken from Austrade's unrestricted international student pivot tables, and cover the entire higher education sector. In 2002, the top three international student markets (China, Malaysia, and Indonesia) accounted for just 35.7% of Australia's much smaller international student enrolments; by 2020, the new top three accounted for 65.4%. Moreover, in 2002 the drop-off between places was gradual, whereas now the drop-off from first to second to third to fourth place (Vietnam) in each case exceeds 50%. Between 2002 and 2020, the Hirschman index of concentration of Australian international student sources rose from 0.26 to 0.44 (the Herfindahl index from 0.07 to 0.20).

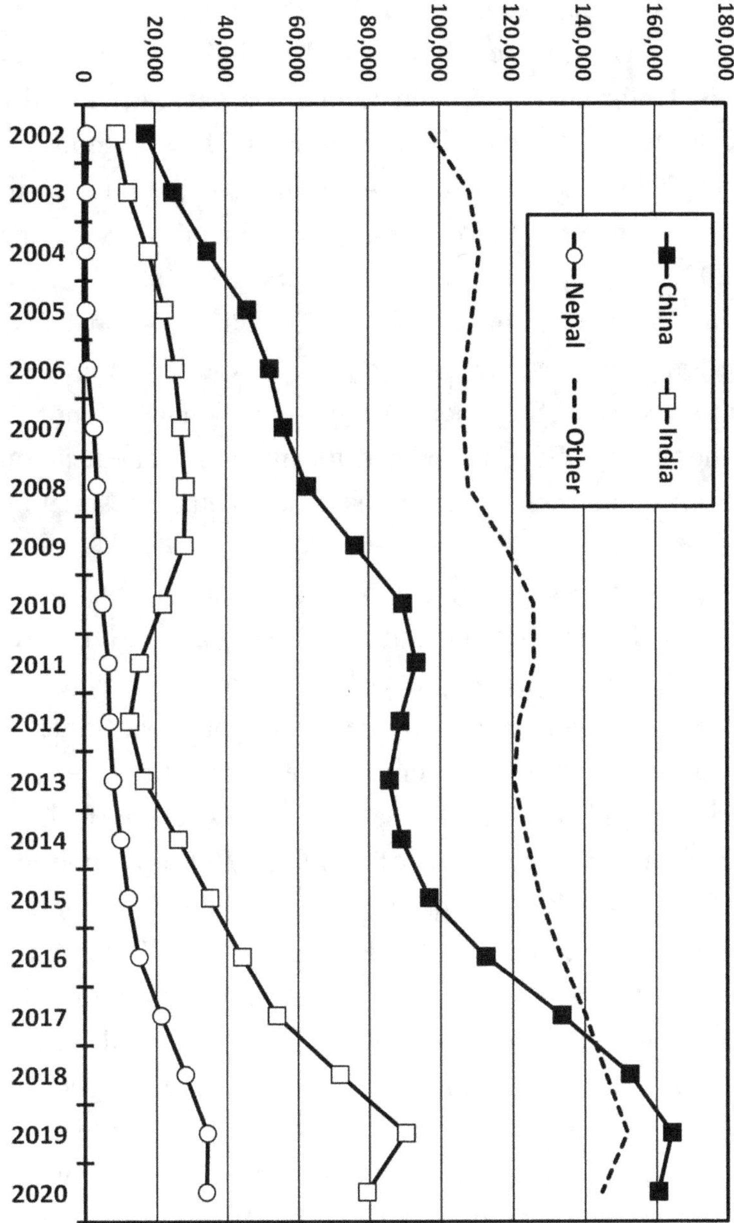

Figure 5. Int'l students in Australia, by country

There are only two ways to bring down those high country concentration levels. Either universities can reduce their intakes from China, India, and Nepal (something they are loath to do), or universities can increase their intakes from other countries. Unfortunately for the second approach, there really is nowhere left to diversify to. In Southeast Asia, Singapore is rich enough to send students to Australia, but the number of Singaporean students in Australia has been in slow decline since 2002. Malaysian student numbers grew slowly until 2011, then declined. Indonesian student numbers have also been in long-term decline. All three of these trends are likely related to the rise of Singapore as the international student hub of Southeast Asia. Even if demand for international education rises in these countries, Singapore is a more natural destination than Australia.

Other countries listed in university strategic plans are Vietnam, the Philippines, Thailand, and Bangladesh. Of these, Vietnam is consistently touted as the best prospect, and it is currently the fourth-largest source of international students in Australia. But it already sends a greater proportion of its population to study in Australia than China does, despite income levels that are only a quarter of China's. With a population of just 95 million (and shrinking), it is unlikely to become a major source of international student growth. The Philippines and Thailand are mature markets. Bangladesh has roughly the same GDP per capita as India, but sends proportionally fewer students to Australia, making it an obvious growth target. Yet even if the number of Bangladeshi international students in Australia were to rise to match Indian per capita levels, it would mean only an additional 4500 students for Australia—out of a (pre-pandemic) international student population of over 440,000. The remaining countries of South and Southeast

Asia are either too small or too poor to supply the requisite numbers of fee-paying students.

There are strong reasons to believe that the large Indian market has already been over-exploited. Income analyses suggest that there are only one-eighth as many families in India who can afford an Australian education for their children as there are Chinese families, yet India sent more than half as many international students to Australia in 2019 as did China.[58] Anecdotal evidence of the financial stress of Indian (and other South Asian) students in Australia abounds. Harder evidence is provided by the dramatic 30% fall in Indian international higher education student numbers in Australia between March 2020 and March 2021. Nepalese and Bangladeshi student numbers were each down 18%, while Sri Lankan numbers fell 22%. Philippine and Thai students down 18% and 20%, respectively. It seems likely that the entire region of developing Asia can provide additional international student flows only on a predatory recruitment basis.

If the Australian university system as a whole suffers from high levels of international student country concentration (and concomitant risk), individual universities are presumably in even worse shape. But unlike their North American and British counterparts, most Australian universities do not break down international student enrolments by country. Estimates can only be compiled from the dribs and drabs contained in occasional newspaper articles, and these reports often do not distinguish between enrolments and EFTSLs, total enrolments or new commencements. The only systematic sources of information are state audit office reports, but these provide very little data, with numbers often obscured by being represented in graphical instead of in tabular form. The NSW audit office is the best of a bad bunch, followed by

Queensland, with others providing virtually no useful data on international student enrolments.

Parsing and combining data from the NSW 2020 audit report, it appears that the highest concentration of students of any nationality at any university in the state (and likely the country) was the 77% of Sydney's international students who came from China, followed by approximately 71% at UNSW.[59] The next highest in the country seem to be Melbourne and Adelaide at 63%, then ANU at 60%, based on data from an unsourced table published by *The Australian*.[60] Several other Australian universities draw between 40% and 60% of their international students from China. It should be noted that these figures are strictly limited to residents of the People's Republic of China; they do not include Chinese students who are permanent residents of Australia or students from Hong Kong, Macao, or Taiwan. Chinese-speaking students from Southeast Asian countries like Singapore are excluded as a matter of course.

The pedagogical problem with market concentration is even more serious than the financial risks that preoccupy government audit offices. When there is one non-native English speaker in a working group of five students, the native speakers may have to 'carry' the non-native linguistically, but the non-native one teaches the others potentially valuable lessons in international teamwork and cross-cultural communication. When native speakers of one particular foreign language (in most cases: Chinese) make up the majority of students in a work group, that exchange breaks down. Many (if not most) Australian universities have already breached such limits in individual classrooms. In fact, many entire courses (particularly in business and journalism) exist primarily to serve Chinese students. This makes a mockery of the whole idea of international education as an exercise in intercultural enrichment. Whatever the optimal number of international students might be from an economic standpoint, it's the educational standpoint that should take precedence.

* * *

How many international students are too many? The answer depends on the perspective. Viewed from a pedagogical perspective, 'too many' international students probably means any number that would place more than one international student in every five-student group. That suggests an upper limit of 20%, which perhaps not coincidentally is roughly the upper bound of international student enrolments at US public universities. Crucially, that one in five students should be spread across multiple countries of origin. It should also be spread across all courses offered by a university, not highly concentrated in one field (i.e., business education). Excessive numbers of international students in business classes don't enrich the educational experiences of nursing or social work students. They only create international ghettos where students struggle to master English or make host-country friends.

Viewed from a financial perspective, 'too many' international students means any number that generates average per-student revenues below the amount paid on behalf of domestic students. Universities have the data and tools to determine this number, but outsiders can only guess at it. There is very strong indirect evidence to suggest that most Australian universities enrol far too many international students. They may not have enough international students to fulfil their revenue ambitions, but they have far too many international students to keep marginal revenues up at the level of average costs. If Australian public universities are determined to admit extraordinary numbers of international students, they should at least increase their international tuition fees to match the average costs of educating domestic students. Ideally, the international fees should be higher.

Even if international students paid higher tuition, the mass admission of international students would only make universities bigger, not better. Australian universities have gotten bigger since the turn of the millennium—much bigger. Total EFTSL across the entire system has increased nearly 80% since 2001, with domestic EFTSL rising by half and international EFTSL tripling. Yet there is little reason to believe that, beyond a certain minimum, bigger is better. Oxford, Cambridge, Harvard, and Stanford all cluster at around 20,000 students by headcount, which would put them in the bottom half among Australian universities. The 10 campuses of the prestigious University of California public system range from 5000 to 45,000 students by headcount. That compares with a Go8 headcount range of 24,000 (UWA) to 87,000 (Monash). The average Go8 headcount of 53,000 students is larger than all but 7 public universities in the entire United States, all but 1 in Canada, and every university in the United Kingdom or New Zealand.

Australia's outsized international enrolments can only be considered a success in commercial terms, and that's the problem. If they scaled back to a little over 10% international by headcount, Australian universities would be ordinary-sized by comparison with their international peers and much better funded on a per-student basis. They could provide a much better education to their domestic Australian students, as well as to the small number of top-quality international students they admitted. But nearly all of their resources would be tied up in teaching and in scholarship engaged in by teachers. They would generate much less free cash flow to be spent at the discretion of the vice chancellor. That free cash flow is the 'profit' we hear so much about, the disposable income that international students make available to vice chancellors. And the vice chancellors don't want to give it up.

Australian universities have relentlessly pursued international students primarily to make discretionary resources available to their management teams. Vice chancellors have spent those resources disproportionately on research; not the ordinary research engaged in by their teaching-and-research academics, but big-ticket research centrally funded by university management. The interpretation that high international enrolments have primarily been used to fund big-ticket research projects (as opposed to being used to plug holes left by inadequate government funding) is backed up by statements made by vice chancellors and industry associations during the coronavirus crisis. They have not pleaded for extra funds to pay teachers, or to keep the lights on. They have pleaded for extra money to support centrally-funded research initiatives.

As explained in *The Conversation* just weeks before the Commonwealth announced $1 billion in supplemental research funding:

Australian university research funding is made up of discretionary income that comes from various sources, including international student fees. This is additional to the funding, including government grants, specifically received for research activities. Universities spent A$12.2 billion on research in 2018. Discretionary income used to fund Australian university research that year amounted to $6 billion, of which $3.1 billion came from international student fees. This means international student fees made up 51% of all the externally sourced research income.[61]

The authors estimated that this put the jobs of "5,100 to 6,100 researchers" at risk, including those of "graduate research students, research assistants and academic research leaders". No mention was made of teachers, or of the ordinary teaching-and-research academics who form the backbone of the university workforce. Similarly, the Go8's CEO has admitted that the coronavirus crisis "has shone an uncomfortable light on what we have known all along—our funding system is broken, with an over-reliance on international fee income to prop up our university research", with Universities Australia's CEO chiming in that "without extra government help" Australia's research capacity would suffer.[62] Of course, these organisations take it for granted that research (divorced from teaching) is a core mission of Australian universities. Again, the HESA and universities' own mission compacts suggest otherwise.

The most straightforward interpretation of the universities' coronavirus funding pleas is probably the correct one: that Australian universities expanded international student enrolments primarily for the purpose of funding additional research, not because of a lack of domestic funding for their ordinary operations. Money is fungible, and Australian universities do not publish detailed budgetary information. Nonetheless, the public statements of Australian university sector leaders make it clear enough how they see the role of international students in the political economy of Australian universities. Australian universities were not forced to turn to international students to make up for Commonwealth underfunding of domestic student places. They chose to expand international student numbers in order to generate free cash flow to fund their vice chancellors' strategic research initiatives.

CHAPTER 4

Is rankings mania warping university priorities?

Throughout the first two decades of the twenty-first century, Australia's universities increasingly redirected international student tuition toward centrally-funded strategic research initiatives. New research centres were established, star academics were recruited to research-only positions, and dedicated research administrators were appointed in unprecedented numbers. Then when international student fee revenue faltered in 2020, the universities appealed for a Commonwealth bailout to shield their new strategic research initiatives from the financial consequences. They succeeded to the tune of $1 billion. The Commonwealth's $1 billion research top-up at the end of 2020 was explicitly targeted toward supporting "research student scholarships, academic salaries, laboratories and research equipment" in an effort to "safeguard thousands of researcher jobs".[63] The very strong implication in the announcement and associated media coverage was that the loss of international students threatened irreparable harm to Australia's research infrastructure.

Money being fungible, it is impossible to trace the $1 billion in emergency research support through to specific research programs. That said, Australian universities have in recent years spawned a plethora of centrally-funded strategic research initiatives that would have been deeply compromised by the loss of the discretionary funds generated by international student fees. These initiatives are not limited to Go8 universities, but they are especially prominent at Go8 universities. At the end of the pre-pandemic boom, there were some 53 identifiable central research initiatives at Go8 universities, focused mainly on the sciences. Although slightly more than half of the Go8's total enrolments are concentrated in non-science disciplines like education, management & commerce, society & culture, and the creative arts, 44 of their 53 strategic initiatives focus on the sciences, with the other 9 primarily focused on the social sciences and area studies. Not a single strategic research initiative at any Go8 university had as its main focus a traditional humanities discipline like history, literature, or philosophy.

Because they are organised very much from the vice chancelleries, not organically rooted in the institutions' ongoing educational missions, Australian universities' strategic initiatives also tend to be highly changeable. Routine website wiping makes it difficult to track the comings and goings of these 'strategic' initiatives, but the University of Melbourne has been more principled about preserving its history than most of its peers, and can thus serve as an example. Out of the five 'Interdisciplinary Research Institutes' founded by Melbourne in 2009, only two remain. In its 2010 annual report, the university promised that "additional interdisciplinary research institutes are planned for development in 2011 in the social sciences, humanities and creative arts".[64] The last two of these either never appeared or were very short-lived. By 2020, Melbourne was back up to five Interdisciplinary Research Institutes, with websites archived for the three disbanded ones. Other universities' strategic initiatives seem to be similarly fleeting, though rarely so well documented.

There is nothing necessarily wrong with changing strategies every few years. But it is indicative of the rootlessness of the supposedly 'strategic' investments made by Australian universities. In the United States, by contrast, most research centres arise from the entrepreneurial initiative and self-organisation of ordinary teaching-and-research academics. They tend to be created from scratch only when a university receives a major special-purpose donation. Moreover, these two mechanisms are often synergistic, with entrepreneurial, bottom-up efforts being nurtured for years by small groups of academics as they search for major donors to fund their growth. The result is an infrastructure of research centres that, at their best, have long institutional lineages, strong connections to the classroom, and high levels of academic buy-in.

In Australia, research—or at least the kind of big-ticket research that vice chancellors like to feature on university websites—tends to be treated as something divorced from teaching, and thus from the ongoing educational mission of the university in general. There is a tendency to unpack the constitution of universities as teaching-and-research institutions into a model of universities as teaching institutions that can be milked to fund research, or even as research institutions that happen to be funded by teaching. Financially, there is no doubt that Australian universities are primarily teaching institutions, with more than 80% of their total revenues tied directly or indirectly to their education missions. But strategically, Australian universities often seem to behave as (and present themselves as) research institutions that engage in education merely as a means to support their research missions.

Thus the drive to recruit international students is commonly framed in terms of the need for funding to support research.[65] In this context, 'research' does not mean the routine scholarship of ordinary teaching-and-research academics. It means the exceptional (and exceptionally expensive) work of 'big science'. This is immediately clear from universities' own estimates of the costs of 'research'. These figures suggest that leading Australian universities produce an average of 4-5 research publications per $1 million of research spending.[66] Were universities to spend that same $1 million to pay four senior business or law professors to engage in research full-time, they could easily quadruple their research outputs. In fact, the typical bare minimum publication expectation for a teaching-and-research scholar at Go8 universities is around 1 publication per year. And that's based on a 40% research loading.

Many education pundits seem not to realise that most of the research engaged in by most teaching-and-research academics receives no explicit funding at all: academics are merely given time to engage in research, and are expected to produce 'research outputs' (i.e., peer-reviewed articles and books) in return. Unfunded or very modestly funded research is the dominant model in the humanities, the social sciences, psychology, business, law, education, mathematics, and the arts. Even many theoretically-oriented engineers and scientists conduct research without receiving any direct funding beyond their salaries. Beyond keeping them employed in the classroom, international student fees contribute very little to their research productivity.

Had Australian universities, like their American counterparts, continued to generate research primarily as a byproduct of employing teaching-and-research academics to undertake their education missions, the 3% decline in student numbers in 2020 would have been experienced as a speed bump for research, not a brick wall. To put it in context, it averages out to a reduction in class size from 100 to 97 students (or the equivalent). Given the continuous churn of academic staff due to retirements and other departures, a decline on that scale could easily have been accommodated by a temporary hiring freeze. And had universities' discretionary research funding been used primarily to support the ongoing research projects of its permanent teaching-and-research academics, a temporary suspension in the internal funding of new projects would have dashed many research dreams, but left most research jobs untouched.

These claims are supported by logic, not by figures, because the figures necessary for supporting such claims are not made public by Australia's public universities. Where does the money for strategic research initiatives come from? We don't know. Do these initiatives represent new, additional research, or just the rebadging of existing, ongoing research? We don't know. Whose jobs are supported by universities' discretionary research funds? We don't know. Whose jobs were saved by the $1 billion in emergency government funding in 2020? We don't know. But a common-sense analysis suggests that universities directed discretionary funds generated by international student fees into strategic research initiatives that employed mainly research-only (i.e., non-teaching) academics and support staff, whose jobs were temporarily saved by the Commonwealth's 2020 intervention. These jobs are now being secured for the future by massive cuts to university teaching academics and support staff going forward.

Pundits have warned that "research rankings and global university reputations are at risk" if "discretionary income used to fund Australian university research" is not restored.[67] Yet as no less an authority than the education minister has pointed out, "the focus on international rankings has led to a relentless drive for international students to fund the larger research volumes that are required to drive up the rankings".[68] There is a strange circular reasoning at work here that has begun to be noticed: "high rankings brought in students, who were willing to pay fees, which in turn funded university operations and especially research, which brought higher rankings".[69] Less noted has been the perverseness of this "virtuous cycle". After all, why should students (international or domestic) bear the burden of financing rankings success, if the researchers they are funding are not the academics who actually teach their classes? And if research does not exist to support a university's educational mission, why should universities (as such) engage in research at all?

Australian rankings success

We live in a scientific age, and it should perhaps come as no surprise that comprehensive universities in which most students enrol in non-scientific subjects would direct most of their strategic attention toward the promotion of big science research initiatives. The prestige of the sciences, once battered by the questioning attitudes of the post-atomic era, has long since recovered to reach new highs in the twenty-first century. And in directing research dollars toward big science, the Go8 and other universities are certainly aligning themselves with government priorities, since the Commonwealth has clearly signaled a preference for science, technology, engineering, and math (STEM) education. But an additional factor contributing to the universities' focus on the sciences may be the disproportionate weighting given to science subjects in international university rankings.

The first organisation to produce a comprehensive international university ranking system was the Center for World-Class Universities of the Institute of Higher Education (later the Graduate School of Education) at Shanghai Jiao

Tong University. Its Academic Ranking of World Universities (ARWU) was first published in 2003. In 2009 the ARWU was commercialised into the ShanghaiRanking Consultancy, which in addition to publishing rankings also offers advisory services to Chinese universities on how to improve their rankings performance. The first major Western university rankings followed a year later. The Times Higher Education - Quacquarelli Symonds World University Rankings (THE-QS) were first published in 2004 by what was then the *Times Higher Education Supplement* in cooperation with the educational consultancy Quacquarelli Symonds, which provided the underlying data. Rounding out the field, the Best Global Universities ranking from *U.S. News & World Report* released its first international league table in 2014.

The ARWU early on made the decision to cover only the sciences and social sciences, not the humanities. According to its creator, the original purpose of the ARWU was "to benchmark top Chinese universities with world-class universities" in the rest of the world.[70] ShanghaiRanking explains on its website that "the initial purpose of ARWU was to find the global standing of top Chinese universities".[71] Thus the ARWU has several distinctive features. The first is its extraordinary focus on prizes. It gives credit for the Nobel Prizes in chemistry, physics, medicine, and economics, plus the Fields Medal in mathematics. It actually evaluates universities' teaching effectiveness solely in terms of the number of these prizes won by their former students. It specifically excludes Nobel Prizes in literature and peace. The ARWU's second distinguishing feature is its high weighting for publications in the journals *Nature* and *Science*. More broadly, it also gives credit for articles published in journals that are covered by the Science Citation Index (SCI) and Social Science Citation Index (SSCI). It gives no credit at all for books.

The THE and QS ranking systems are more balanced. The two organisations published joint rankings until 2009, but since 2010 have published separate rankings. Both THE and QS operate educational consultancy businesses, but THE's core audience is academics, while QS targets mainly students. These differing emphases are reflected in the two organisations' rankings approaches, with THE giving greater weight to research and QS giving greater weight to teaching. Both, however, attempt to cover the full range of academic disciplines, weighting their results by the number of academic staff that universities employ in each area. Due to technical limitations, however, neither includes books, which are the mainstay of academic publishing in the humanities. Among major ranking systems, the *U.S. News* Best Global Universities is the only one to include a (tiny) weighting for book publications. A methodological breakdown of all four ranking systems is provided in Table 9.

The four major international ranking systems differ dramatically in their composition, yet produce broadly similar results. World-famous universities like Harvard, Stanford, Oxford, Cambridge, and MIT figure in the global Top 10 in all four systems, although their specific positions differ. Below the Top 10, however, individual universities are separated by relatively small differences in raw scores on each of the rankings, producing wide variability in results. To take just one example of a famous university that hovers on the edge of the global Top 10, the placements for the Johns Hopkins University range from #10 on the *U.S. News* rankings to #25 on the QS rankings. The variability for non-US universities can be even greater. For example, the University of Tokyo pips Johns Hopkins on the QS (#23), but lags far behind on the *U.S. News* ranking (#73).

Table 9. Methodologies of international ranking systems

Component	ARWU	THE	QS	US News
Teaching				
Teaching reputation		15.00%	20.00%	
Employability reptation			10.00%	
Teacher / student ratio		4.50%	20.00%	
Staff with doctoral degrees		6.00%		
Doctoral degrees granted		2.25%		
Nobel prizes (alumni)	10.00%			
Total teaching	**10.00%**	**27.75%**	**50.00%**	**0.00%**
Research				
Research reputation		18.00%	20.00%	25.00%
Citation metrics	20.00%	30.00%	20.00%	50.00%
Research grant income		8.50%		
Article publications	20.00%	6.00%		10.00%
Articles in Nature/Science	20.00%			
Conference papers				2.50%
Book publications				2.50%
Nobel prizes (staff)	20.00%			
Total research	**80.00%**	**62.50%**	**40.00%**	**90.00%**
Internationalisation				
Int'l research collaboration		2.50%		10.00%
International faculty		2.50%	5.00%	
International students		2.50%	5.00%	
Total internationalisation	**0.00%**	**7.50%**	**10.00%**	**10.00%**
Size adjustments				
Per capita output	10.00%			
University revenues		2.25%		
Total size adjustments	**10.00%**	**2.25%**	**0.00%**	**0.00%**
Sum totals:	**100.00%**	**100.00%**	**100.00%**	**100.00%**

Table 10. International rankings of Go8 universities

University	ARWU	THE	QS	US News
Adelaide	101-150	118	108	73
ANU	76	59	27	64
Melbourne	33	31	37	25
Monash	80	64	58	48
Queensland	51	62	47	36
Sydney	69	51	38	27
UNSW	65	67	43	51
UWA	96	139	93	79
Nominal date:	"2021"	"2022"	"2022"	"2021"
Release date:	Aug-21	Sep-21	Jun-21	Oct-20

Australia's Go8 universities perform remarkably well on all four systems. Their most recent rankings are reported in Table 10. The six strongest Go8 universities place in the global 'Top 100' in all four systems, and all eight make it in the 'Top 100' in the *U.S. News* rankings. The median Go8 positions on the THE and ARWU rankings are charted in Figure 6. All Go8 universities except ANU have risen dramatically in the science-heavy ARWU rankings since they were first introduced in 2003. They have fared less well in the more-comprehensive THE rankings, though mainly due to a major methodological shift in 2010 that saw all except Adelaide and Melbourne tumble. Allowing for changes in methods, most Go8 universities have held just about stable on the British THE rankings, while slowly climbing up the Chinese ARWU table.

Australia is the 54th largest country in the world by population, the 14th in the size of its economy, and the 10th by income per capita (more or less, depending on the statistical sources chosen). But it is a heavy hitter in the university sweepstakes, home to six, seven, or even eight of the world's

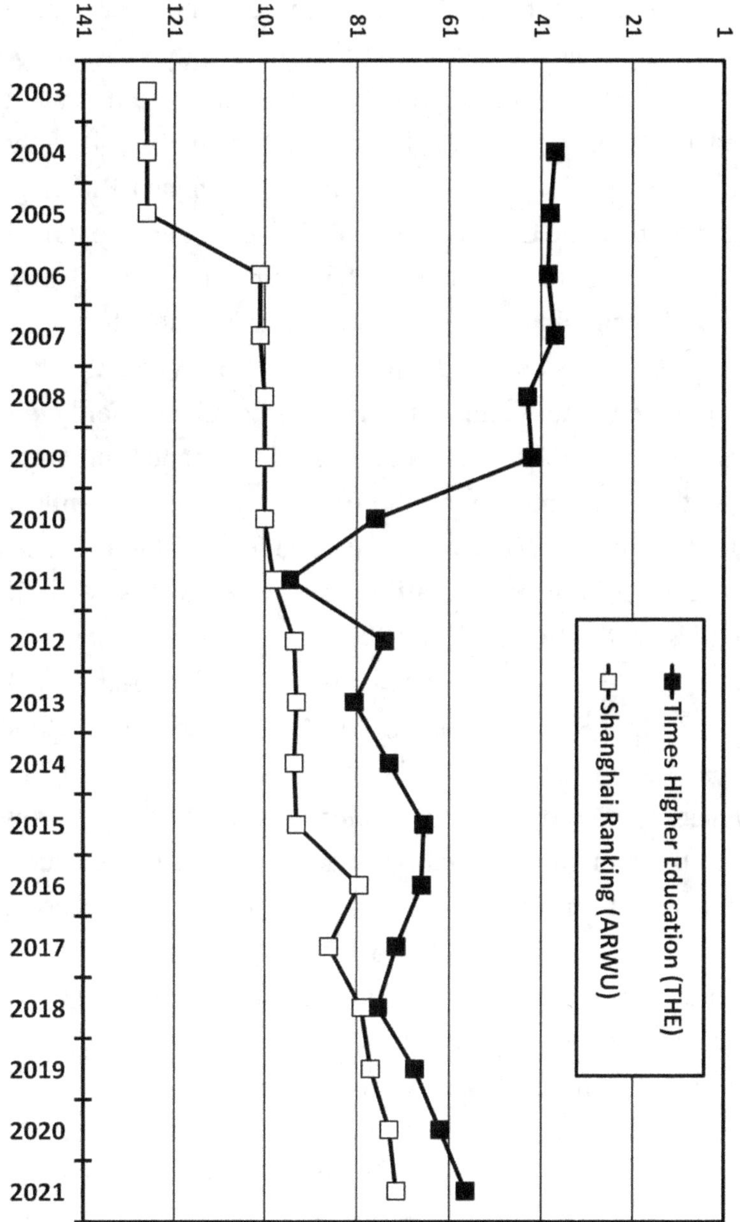

Figure 6. Median ranking of Go8 universities

'Top 100' universities. On all four international ranking systems, Australia sits firmly in 3rd place in the world its total number of Top 100 universities, trailing only the US and UK. What's more, Australia leads the world with 14 universities in the Top 100 on the THE Young University Rankings for universities founded in the last 50 years. Even more incredibly, 4 of the Top 10 universities in the world on the THE Impact Rankings (loosely based on the UN's Sustainable Development Goals) are Australian. Taken at face value, all that sounds like a good news story, one that should put paid to the 'cultural cringe' forever.

Did a little deeper, and questions arise. When the first international rankings came out in 2003, Australia had only two universities in the global Top 100: the ANU (#49) and Melbourne (#92), with the country as a whole ranking a distant ninth in the world on the ARWU. Australia's two Top 100 universities left it tied with France and trailing the United States (with 58 universities in the global Top 100), the United Kingdom (9), Germany (5), Japan (5), Canada (4), the Netherlands (3), Sweden (3), and Switzerland (3). The ARWU rankings method has remained almost unchanged over the system's 18-year run, and is heavily biased toward the sciences. The ARWU entirely excludes the humanities, creative arts, law, and most business disciplines. Thus in just two decades, Australia went from being a relative science lightweight to far outproducing scientific giants like China, Germany, and Japan. How did such a small country manage such a startling transformation?

Vanity of vanities, all is vanity, but few things more so than international university rankings. Closely watched and aggressively pursued by university vice chancellors, they do little to measure the educational outcomes that really matter for students. They disregard domestic educational priorities entirely and instead rank universities based on whatever international data happen to be available. This is in stark contrast to the original purpose of university rankings. Domestic American university rankings were first produced by *U.S. News* in 1983. They have always focused on student-centred metrics like graduation and retention rates (35% weighting), undergraduate reputation (20%), class size and other teaching metrics (20%), admissions selectivity (7%), financial resources (13%), and graduate financial success (5%).[72] Research output hardly figures in these rankings, because research is viewed as a byproduct of the universities' educational missions, not a major goal of the universities as such.

Universities that aspire to climb the domestic *U.S. News* rankings must engage in the hard managerial work of recruiting the best students and ensuring their success by keeping class sizes down and providing adequate support services. The international rankings, by contrast, focus heavily on research productivity, because article citation metrics are internationally comparable and readily available from commercial data providers. The *U.S. News* domestic reputational survey is also well-designed as a survey instrument, with academics rating only those institutions with which they have had personal experience. In the THE and QS international surveys, by contrast, academics are asked to nominate personal 'Top 10' lists of regional and global competitors. The survey-takers seem not to realise the circularity of this process: the only way most academics have to know which have the best teaching in the world is to consult the rankings.

Instead of focusing on teaching-focused domestic rankings like their American counterparts, Australian universities have embraced the research-focused international rankings. This accounts for (or at least reinforces) the dominance of big science in Go8 strategic initiatives. It also accounts for the decision of many Australian universities to sacrifice their educational missions during the coronavirus crisis in order to maintain funding for their flagship scientific research programs. As the old management maxim has it, 'what gets measured gets done', and when it comes to the international rankings, it's scientific research that gets measured. Thus while American universities have been incentivised by their own domestic rankings to focus on improvements in education, Australian universities, by pursuing international rankings, are actually incentivised to raid educational budgets to fund scientific research.

Gaming the rankings game

The American domestic university rankings cannot easily be gamed: the only way to improve a university's ranking is for its management to improve the university's actual performance. But the international rankings are much more ... malleable. The margins separating universities below the global 'Top Ten' are so narrow that something as small as an individual hiring decision can move a university several places in the rankings. For example, when an ANU professor (and future vice chancellor) shared one-quarter of the Nobel Prize for physics in 2011, his university jumped six places in the ARWU rankings. Any university lucky enough to employ an unshared Nobel Prize winner might climb a dozen spots or more.

Perhaps foreseeing the possibility their rankings might spark a bidding war for Nobel Laureates, the ShanghaiRanking Consultancy awards ARWU points only to the institution that employed the winner at the time of the award. But the ARWU has another lever that is more susceptible to manipulation: the number of staff members who appear on the annual Highly Cited Researcher (HCR) list compiled by Clarivate Analytics. University employment of academics on this finite list of 6,389 researchers accounts for 20% of the ARWU. Membership in the Clarivate HCR list is based on the citation counts of journal articles indexed in the Science Citation Index (SCI) and Social Science Citation Index (SSCI), which also separately contribute to the ARWU rankings. Thus the recruitment of a Clarivate HCR represents thus represents a real bonanza for ARWU rankings success.

Recruiting a Clarivate HCR pulls the citation levers on the other three ranking systems as well, though not as strongly as it influences the ARWU. Moreover, HCR recruitment can reasonably be presented as an entirely appropriate university behaviour: what sane university would not want to recruit one of the world's most highly cited researchers? Nonetheless, outright bidding for the services of HCRs turned into a scandal in 2011, when *Science* magazine broke the news that two Saudi universities were abusing the list to enhance their international rankings.[73] They were paying HCRs to add their universities as 'secondary affiliations' on their Clarivate profiles. As a result, these relatively unknown universities were catapulted to ARWU success, with individual departments hitting the global Top Ten in their narrow disciplinary rankings.

This 'secondary affiliation' loophole was later closed by the ARWU, but HCR abuses persist. Two Saudi universities continue to rank in the top thirty globally by number of HCRs, but web searches of the scholars who got them there suggest that many of them do not actually work in Saudi Arabia. Instead, they work at low-ranked universities in other countries that are not in the running for a high ARWU ranking, and thus presumably do not closely monitor their scholars' affiliations as recorded by Clarivate. Some find nothing wrong with this kind of reputation-for-hire behaviour. A Cambridge University HCR astronomer told *Science* quite openly that "universities buy people's reputations all the time. In principle, this is no different from Harvard hiring a prominent researcher".

But if there's one place in the world that is aggressively recruiting HCRs, it's not Harvard. It's Australia. Around 2014, Australian universities began a dramatic increase in their numbers of Clarivate-recognised HCRs. Between 2014 and 2020, the proportion of the world's HCRs based in Australia more than doubled, from 2.02% to 4.77%. Harvard's proportion, by contrast, has been stable at around 3% for the last two decades. Table 11 reports the numbers of HRCs in Australia and in the world as a whole over the period 2004-2020, taking into account primary affiliations only. Data from 2001 and from 2014 onward have been downloaded directly from Clarivate. With the exception of the 2001 list, Clarivate no longer makes pre-2014 data available, and the missing years' lists do not seem to have been archived anywhere online. Nonetheless, it was possible to source the 2004 and 2007 results from published research papers, allowing these two years to be included in the table.[74]

Given that the absolute number of HCRs in the world has tended to increase over time, it's no surprise that the number in Australia has increased as well. But the rising proportion of the world's HCRs that are affiliated with Australian institutions tells another story. In its 2018 and 2019 HCR press releases, Clarivate honoured Australia as one of only three countries (alongside China and the United States) receiving detailed commentary. In both years, Clarivate wrote that "Australian research institutions appear to have recruited a significant number of Highly Cited Researchers since 2014 while also increasing their number of homegrown Highly Cited Researchers". The 2020 release merely noted that "Australia is powering ahead".

Table 11. Highly cited researchers (HCRs)

Year	Australia	World	AUS%
2001	112	7033	1.59%
-- Gap in the available data --			
-- New methodology introduced --			
2004	78	4569	1.71%
-- Gap in the available data --			
2007	105	5790	1.81%
-- Gap in the available data --			
-- New methodology introduced --			
2014	65	3215	2.02%
2015	103	3126	3.29%
2016	115	3266	3.52%
2017	127	3538	3.59%
2018	170	4058	4.19%
-- New methodology introduced --			
2018	245	6079	4.03%
2019	271	6216	4.36%
2020	305	6389	4.77%

Absent an unlikely self-confession from the universities involved, it is impossible to know whether Australian universities were "powering ahead" through hard-won improvements in research management or through the application of free cash flow to give academics time off from teaching and buy in talent from overseas. The rankings trajectories of Go8 universities, however, illustrates how important HCR counts can be. Between 2003 and 2017, Melbourne increased its ARWU HCR subscore from 14.5 points to 45.0 points (out of a possible 100 points). Over that period, its ARWU rank rose from #98 to #39 in the world. The ANU, by contrast, went the opposite direction, with its HCR subscore declining from 44.7 to 15.4. Its ranking fell from #49 to #97.

The direction (or redirection) of limited university resources toward supporting their most successful researchers might sound reasonable, even laudable, to the uninitiated. But researchers who have been liberated from the classroom contribute very little to universities' core educational missions. There are also more subtle problems in the way research 'success' is measured. At first glance, the recruitment of HCRs sounds meritocratic and value-neutral. But Clarivate only indexes HRCs in 21 broad fields of study, nearly all of them scientific. Only two non-scientific fields are indexed by Clarivate (Economics & Business and Social Sciences), and no humanities fields whatsoever. Even this limited non-science coverage is less than it seems. All 9 of Australia's 2020 'Social Sciences' HCRs (and there are only 9) are public health researchers. In fact, only one out of Australia's 305 HCRs is not a scientist of some kind, and even that person is an 'Economics & Business' HCR who specialises in econometrics (i.e., statistics).

By focusing resources on HCRs—whether through strategic recruitment or by making strategic investments in their most promising researchers—Australian universities are, in effect, tilting the academic playing field toward the sciences. No matter how hard they work and how many accolades they receive, no one in the humanities and virtually no one in the social sciences, business, law, education, or the arts is ever going to be an HCR. More consequential than that inherent unfairness is the irony that the most effective way to attract, create, and retain HCRs is to liberate them from teaching. Many of the HCR scientists employed by Australian universities will never teach in an Australian classroom. Even granting that those researchers nonetheless somehow contribute to the overall welfare of Australia, it is not at all clear that housing them in universities is the best way to attract them and fund their work.

Research versus scholarship

The rapid expansion in international student fee revenue in the 2000s and 2010s gave Australia's universities the freedom to set their own research priorities, unfettered by government or societal oversight, and delinked from student demand. They seem to have used that freedom to invest heavily in big science and scientific HCRs. It is impossible to trace individual dollars through university accounts, but the proliferation of big science research initiatives and the tripling in Australia's proportion of the world's HCRs since the turn of the millennium point strongly in that direction. So do the universities' warnings that the loss of international students due to coronavirus travel restrictions threatened their capacity to engage in world-class scientific research.

Nonetheless, despite two decades of rapid growth in international student fee revenue, most Australian university research is still funded by the Commonwealth. And the requirement that Commonwealth-supported teachers also be scholars forces universities to fund their research efforts with at least some regard for relative student enrolments across disciplines. But the HESA does not actually require that Commonwealth grant funding be dedicated to supporting the research of universities' teacher-scholars, and the apportionment of the Commonwealth's research block grant funding is not tied to teaching at all. Despite the fact that these grants are only made available to institutions that engage in teaching, the Commonwealth's approach to research funding has evolved to focus almost entirely on rewarding success in gaining research grants.

Direct Commonwealth support for university research dates back to 1936, and has always been focused on the sciences.[75] Since 2017, the Commonwealth has funded university research through two main block grant mechanisms, each allocating around $1 billion per year: the Research Training Program (RTP) to fund postgraduate research (primarily PhD) students and the Research Support Program (RSP) to fund overhead on research grants. Universities receive RTP block grants on the basis of past research student completions (50%), success in nationally-competitive grants programs (25%), and success in obtaining other grants (25%). They receive RSP block grants on the basis of success in nationally-competitive grants programs (47%), and success in obtaining other grants (53%). The late-2020 supplemental grant of $1 billion for university research was delivered via the RSP by roughly doubling universities' RSP allotments for 2021.

It is a trope of university complaints about the inadequacy of Commonwealth research funding that "federal mechanisms designed to cover the indirect costs are increasingly inadequate".[76] In 2020, the RSP provided $428 million to support indirect costs on the basis of 'Category 1' nationally-competitive grants totaling $1.8 billion in 2019, for an implicit indirect cost rate of just 24%. For comparison, the average indirect cost ceiling for US government grants, which is negotiated separately by each institution, is often reported to be 52%.[77] That seems to make Australia look positively stingy, but the comparison is not quite accurate. Although American universities have negotiated indirect cost ceilings averaging 52%, their actual reimbursement rates for indirect costs on US government grants average only 34%.[78] In Japan and the European Union, indirect cost recovery rates are even lower, at 30% and 25%, respectively. Australia falls short, but just short, of these levels.

Broadening the scope, in addition to its support for indirect costs on nationally-competitive government grants, the remaining $482 million of RSP funding is allocated on the basis of Category 2 (non-competitive government), Category 3 (private industry, foundation, and international), and Category 4 (public-private cooperative research centre) grants. Such grants generally do not attract indirect cost support in other countries— certainly not Category 3 grants, which make up 41% of all non-competitive grants in Australia. Strip out Category 3 grants, and the implicit RSP support for the indirect costs of government Category 2 and 4 grants is 22%.

Australia's funding of indirect costs on Category 1, 2, and 4 government grants combined averages out to 23%, which seems low by international standards. But these comparisons omit one crucial factor. On top of its RSP support, Australia's RTP funds the costs of most domestic PhD study in Australia. This is internationally unparalleled. In the US, major research universities generally pay the tuition of research students out of general funds. In the European Union, research students are generally funded out of the direct costs of grants. And in Japan, research students are generally expected to pay tuition fees. Australia's RTP funding of more than $1 billion per year provides grant-funded research projects with research students essentially cost-free. Allocating even a small portion of RTP funding for PhD students to the indirect costs of government grants would raise Australian government grant funding levels well above international standards.

Funding for direct costs is much harder to compare, given the enormous disparities in the structure of grant funding across countries. At the broadest level, funding for the US National Science Foundation is 13 times that of the Australian Research Council (ARC), exactly in line with the relative population sizes of the two countries. The main difference is that the ARC and other Australian funding bodies allocate much more of their resources to funding academic salaries via fellowships and teaching buy-outs, instead of directly funding research as such. The US National Science Foundation, by contrast, does not generally offer academic fellowships.

In a strange twist of university accounting, an ARC or other government-sponsored fellowship has the power to transform an ordinary scholar into a formally-recognised 'researcher'. Australian universities, trade associations, education pundits, and even the government itself often recognise as 'research' only activities that are explicitly funded by a research grant. Stranger still, all PhD students are by statute defined as researchers, even if their PhD supervisors are not—except when they are actively supervising PhD research. This is all quite confused in the relevant documentation, but TEQSA clarifies in a draft guidance note the difference between high-prestige 'research' and the mere 'scholarship' of ordinary academics. For TEQSA, scholarship is a set of "activities concerned with advances in knowledge" while research is "a sub-set of the various types of scholarship that is limited to generating new knowledge".[79]

Officially, the Australian government defines 'research' as "Research and Experimental Development as defined in the Frascati Manual 2015 maintained by the Organisation for Economic Cooperation and Development".[80] The OECD's definition, however, is highly restrictive. It limits research to "creative and systematic work undertaken in order to increase the stock of knowledge ... and to devise new applications of available knowledge".[81] To qualify as research, an activity must simultaneously be "novel, creative, uncertain, systematic, [and] transferable and/or reproducible".[82] That's a tall order, and one that is not met by much of what academics think of as their research activities—or what the government classifies as research outputs. Nonetheless, the OECD's latest Frascati

Manual assures readers that its definitions, developed in the context of science and engineering, can be applied without revision to the humanities and social sciences. It offers the helpful example that historians might "study the history and human impact of glacial outburst floods in a country".[83]

Well they might. But most historians are more likely to study history. When they do, or when literary scholars interrogate a text, or for that matter when accountants opine on the proper interpretation of an accounting rule, are they engaging in research? From TEQSA's perspective, the answer is probably no. For TEQSA, research is inextricably linked with knowledge, as such: "TEQSA defines research as 'academic activities ... that contribute to new knowledge through original investigation'".[84] Opinion, interpretation, exegesis, and understanding are forms of scholarship, but do not constitute knowledge, as such. The same might be said of most of what passes for science, but scientific opinion is much more easily stamped with the imprimatur of knowledge.

* * *

Is rankings mania warping university priorities? Australian universities (and particularly Go8 universities) have vastly expanded the scale of their big science research programs over the last two decades, and that has been reflected in their march up the Shanghai ARWU rankings. Many non-Go8 universities are also highly ranked, if not in the global Top 100 then at least in the next tier. For them, too, science is the key. Science and scientific subjects may account for only a third or so of university staff and students, but they absorb the preponderance of public, government, and rankings attention. Far from seeing this science fetish as a problem, most commentators are quite happy to see universities focus on scientific research, and unquestioningly embrace the wildly disproportionate weighting of the sciences in international university rankings.

The conflation of scientific research with research *tout court* is reflected in the very language that TEQSA and other government organs use when discussing the role of research in the modern research university. The appropriation of the prestigious label 'research' by the sciences and the concomitant demotion of most other forms of academic inquiry to the more flexible category 'scholarship' did not occur overnight, nor did it occur only in Australia. It harks back to the 'two cultures' debate of the middle of the twentieth century, and even earlier to the *Methodenstreit* (methods dispute) of late nineteenth century German social science. At a deep epistemological level, the gap between the sciences and the humanities is fundamentally unbridgeable. Scientific research offers answers that, although often false, are at least falsifiable; humane scholarship offers understandings that can only ever be more or less meaningful, not more or less correct.

The language of 'research', originally the preserve of the sciences, has come to be applied to the entire university, with the result that traditional humanities 'scholarship' has been devalued. In Australia, throughout the OECD, and especially in China, 'research' has come to mean 'scientific research', sometimes supplemented by those forms of social science research that most closely copy scientific paradigms. Thus the strategic research initiatives of Go8 universities are (almost all) focused on science disciplines; international university rankings are (disproportionately) science rankings; social science HCRs are (in practice) scientists; definitions of research are (overwhelmingly) modeled on scientific methods. And perennially concerned that too few students choose to study science, the Commonwealth always stands ready to subsidise science education, reinforcing its longstanding bias toward funding scientific research.

In the twentieth century, the humanities and social sciences held their own, and even flourished, because research was tied to teaching, and students continued to study non-science subjects. In the twenty-first century, however, international rankings have tipped the balance—at least in Australia. Over the last two decades, Australian universities have successfully clawed their way up the international rankings by using teaching revenues generated by non-science disciplines (especially business) to subsidise scientific research. International ranking systems did not create the academic bias in favour of science, but they exacerbated it, by giving universities that were able to generate free cash flow a strong incentive to invest it in science.

The government (and indeed the public) may be sanguine about this. Big science is more prestigious than ever, and few outside the humanities and social sciences mourn its growing dominance. But some may eventually come to ask, regarding the rise of the sciences and the rankings success it has fueled: what's in it for Australia? The mass production of highly-cited journal articles by centrally-funded, research-only scientists is great for vice chancellors' bragging rights, and perhaps their pay packages. It's also great for the careers of those few lucky scientists who receive funding support. But any benefits for Australian students are tangential at best, since the more resources go into scientific research, the fewer high-flying scientists actually teach students.

The fact that only teaching institutions are eligible to receive funding through Australian government research block grants is a compelling reminder that the Commonwealth's primary interest in funding university research is to fund the research of teacher-scholars. Historically, the impetus for the

Commonwealth funding of scientific research arose out of the fact that the research of teacher-scholars in the sciences was much more expensive than that of teacher-scholars in the humanities. Without additional government funding for the research of science teachers, universities would have had to abandon teaching science. It is necessary and natural that the lion's share of government research block grants should go to the sciences. But it should be funding scientists who teach. That was the historical purpose of Commonwealth research block grants, and it makes a lot of sense.

In recent years, all of this has become thoroughly confused. The division of Commonwealth funding streams into per-student grants and supplemental research grants has combined with historical amnesia to produce an emerging consensus that the Commonwealth Grant Scheme supports teaching, while research grants and research block grants fund research. This (mis-) understanding is a convenient one for university administrators, since it allows them to portray research as being desperately underfunded, thus supporting demands for more money. The long-term consequences of this stance are, however, potentially disastrous for the future of universities. After all, if research funding is permanently divorced from teaching, why should governments restrict research grants to universities, instead of opening them up for public tender? And why should governments fund basic research at all?

The pursuit of international rankings success, particularly (but not exclusively) among Go8 universities, has warped Australian higher education in ways that will take decades to reverse—if it is reversed at all. Australia really does have at least six universities that are among the world's 100 most productive research institutions, and Australia really is home to nearly 5% of the world's most accomplished research scientists.

There is nothing fake about Australia's rankings success. Had it been achieved organically, through the careful shepherding of resources and the effective management of academic staff, it would represent an impressive accomplishment. But Australian rankings success has not been achieved; it has been bought. It is based on redirecting money that was collected to fund education (which includes supporting the research of teacher-scholars) toward the funding of rankings-eligible research outputs. That makes sense in the perverse economy of university prestige. It probably does not make sense for Australia, its government, or its students.

CHAPTER 5

Have Australia's universities been corrupted by China?

One of the biggest challenges in management theory is goal alignment: how to ensure that the goals of managers are aligned with the goals of proprietors. In the private sector, a common solution is to link executive remuneration to a company's share price. Another is to link executive remuneration to financial targets, like profitability, revenue growth, or cost cutting. In most countries (including Australia), listed companies are required not only to disclose the overall level of executive remuneration, but also to disclose the terms of any such performance-linked incentives that might influence executive decision-making. The idea is to give investors insights into the drivers of executive behaviour, and to assure them that executives are properly incentivised to act in the best interests of shareholders.

Executive compensation terms at Australia's public universities, by contrast, are secretive and opaque. The total pay packages of vice chancellors and other senior executives are published, along with the total amounts of any performance-linked bonuses, but the triggers for those bonuses are generally kept confidential. Where the Australian Securities and Investments Commission has blazed a path toward accountability and transparency, TEQSA and state regulators fear to tread. As a result, the Australian public knows more about the drivers of executive behaviour at its listed companies than at its public universities. It took a whistleblower leak for even a federal senator to learn the terms of a vice chancellor's compensation incentives at the University of Queensland—and even he could only disclose those terms under parliamentary privilege.[85]

The University of Queensland key performance indicator revealed at the time was that the vice chancellor should "work towards a sound and strategic positioning in China, given its potential rise towards becoming the predominant provider of research globally and that it will continue to be a very important source of international students".[86] Its revelation provoked controversy because the vice chancellor was awarded a performance bonus despite failing to diversify the university away from its high level of reliance on Chinese international students. Queensland's coronavirus-induced financial crisis ensured that international student fee revenue would grab the headlines. This obscured the real bombshell: the expectation that the vice chancellor should "work towards a sound and strategic positioning in China" due to China's importance as a "provider of research". This is a much more compromising revelation than anything to do with an overreliance on Chinese students.

It is true that many Australian universities (especially, but not exclusively, Go8 universities) are indeed highly dependent on Chinese international student fee revenue, some of them for as much as one-quarter of their total revenues from all sources.[87] But this revenue stream is, under ordinary circumstances, not directly influenced by relations between individual universities and the Chinese government. In fact, China has never previously 'weaponised' student flows as a tool of international relations, despite many threats to do so.[88] There is even less evidence to suggest that it has ever steered students away from individual universities in an attempt to influence their behaviour. This may have happened, or (more likely) universities might fear that it could happen, but it is not a major factor in universities' relationships with China.

Universities' research relationships with China, by contrast, are much more thoroughly politicised. For example, the US Ivy League's Cornell University was forced to suspend research collaboration with a Chinese counterpart in 2015 due to Chinese government harassment.[89] The program involved sensitive research into workers' rights in China. Few Australian universities are so courageous. Research sponsored by the ANU's Centre on China in the World sponsors research in five areas that range from the uncontroversial ('Sustainable Urbanisation' and 'Energy Transition') to the celebratory (a 'Politics, Policy and Society' program that will investigate the "adaptations in public policy [that] are driving China's re-emergence as a world power").[90] Until recently, the University of Sydney's China Studies Centre focused on "climate change, health services, cultural heritage and new technologies".[91] The Australia-China Relations Institute (ACRI) at UTS focuses on trade and investment. Late to the game, in 2018 UNSW opened a research centre in China "dedicated to environmental protection".[92]

Unlike Cornell's research into working conditions in China, none of these Australian initiatives is likely to make waves. Individual scholars at each of these universities, and even some who are associated with their respective China studies centres, may conduct research that is critical of China. That research may even, in some cases, be funded by the centres—though it is unlikely to be foregrounded on their websites. Contrary to some public perceptions, Australian universities do not systematically suppress research that is critical of China, and academic freedom is alive and well in Australia.[93] The China threat to Australian research autonomy is much more subtle than the media portrays. Despite a handful of ham-fisted attempts to quash criticism, it consists mainly of initiatives not pursued, academics not hired, and research not funded. The strategic research initiatives of Australian universities are just that—strategic. No Australian university is likely to consider it strategic to use discretionary funds to support research that is highly critical of China.

It's hard to manufacture a conspiracy out of avenues not pursued, and thus it is very difficult to substantiate claims of undue Chinese influence over the behaviour of Australian universities. Yet the absence of evidence is not evidence of absence. Quite the contrary: what universities choose to keep quiet or confidential about their relationships with China may point to unpalatable realities that lurk just below the surface. The culture of secrecy surrounding many universities' dealings with China is suspiciously not palpable. University participation in Chinese initiatives like the Confucius Institutes and the Thousand Talents programs is often cloaked in confidentiality when it could be highly publicised, and likely would be, if it involved any country other than China. It sometimes almost seems as if universities are ashamed of their relationships with China, and believe that the less said about them, the better.

The silence that surrounds Australian universities' China ties breeds suspicion—and rightly so, since it is the ideal environment for the behind-the-scenes exercise of inappropriate Chinese influence. Politicians, the press, and the public have become alert to the possibility that Australia's universities might be compromised by their China ties, but they are often poorly equipped to understand the inner workings of universities and the obscure routes through which Chinese influence can operate. Worse, they may have little understanding of exactly why and how universities might be corrupted by China. As a result, compromising information often hides in plain sight, since those who are responsible for holding universities accountable are unaware that the information is, in fact, compromising. Unfortunately, the sparse data that universities have allowed into the public domain cannot support a meaningful statistical analysis of China's influence on Australian universities. Nonetheless, enough information is available to at least shed some light on the problem, and its potential solutions.

Australia's Foreign Relations Act and the Confucius Institutes

The threat posed by China to the integrity of Australian institutions has become a staple of media reporting over the last five years, and universities have been at the forefront of the debate. In November 2019, the Commonwealth and the universities agreed a set of unenforceable 'Guidelines to Counter Foreign Interference in the Australian University Sector', while in 2020 the Parliamentary Joint Committee on Intelligence and Security opened an inquiry into 'National Security Risks Affecting the Australian Higher Education and Research Sector'. The former did little more than define foreign interference and urge universities to 'be mindful' of risks and undertake 'due diligence' while maintaining 'transparent and robust reporting'.[94] The latter was supposed to report in July 2021, but as of October 1 had still not done so.

In a potentially more consequential intervention, at the end of 2020 the Commonwealth passed legislation to counter inappropriate foreign influence in the conduct of international relations at the sub-national level. The Australia's Foreign Relations Act (AFRA) primarily targeted state, territory, and local governments, which were required to declare their agreements with their international peers. This included everything from mundane sister city programs up to Victoria's headline 'Belt and Road' agreement with China's National Development and Reform Commission. The AFRA was also made to apply to universities, requiring them to declare any "written arrangement, agreement, contract, understanding or undertaking" with a foreign government or a foreign university that "does not have institutional autonomy". The obvious intention of this convoluted language was to force Australian universities to declare their partnerships in China.

Australian universities were required to report their existing agreements to the government by June 10, 2021. They reportedly declared "more than 6000" agreements, with "more than 4000" declared by Go8 universities and "more than 2000" by others.[95] At time of writing, the agreements had not yet been published in the public registry set up by the legislation, but it hardly matters: the public registry will include only the title of and parties to the agreement, and whether or not the minister for foreign affairs decided to annul it. Nor is the government itself likely to learn much about these agreements, if Victoria's Belt & Road agreement is anything to go by. Annulled on April 21, the state of Victoria's memorandum of understanding and framework agreement to support China's Belt & Road Initiative contained nothing but non-binding platitudes about friendship and cooperation. Many university agreements are likely to amount to much the same.

It is possible that the foreign minister will decide to annul some university agreements, but this has little potential to thwart inappropriate Chinese influence. Like Victoria's Belt & Road agreement, most formal university agreements with their Chinese counterparts are likely to be innocuous and unenforceable memoranda of understanding. Chinese institutions have a penchant for signing ceremonies and other symbolic gestures, and it is almost certain that many of the thousands of Australian university agreements registered under the AFRA are nothing more than dead letters. The real compromises lie elsewhere. The root problem with the Australian government's approach to countering Chinese influence is that it focuses on formal agreements that have the potential to cause embarrassment instead of on the informal understandings that underlie them. By focusing only on formal, written agreements, the AFRA is designed to overlook the real mechanisms through which Chinese influence operates.

One clear target of the AFRA is Australia's 13 university-based Confucius Institutes.[96] China sponsors hundreds of Confucius Institutes around the world, most of them based at universities (although individual institutional arrangements differ). Until 2019, the NSW Department of Education even had a Confucius Institute agreement to deliver Chinese language education in 13 NSW schools. The NSW agreement was apparently made directly with the Chinese government's Office of Chinese Language Council International (known as the 'Hanban' or 'Chinese Institute').[97] The university agreements typically involve an Australian university, a Chinese partner university, and the Hanban, with the Chinese university providing teaching staff and the Hanban making a financial contribution. The university-based Confucius Institutes are constituted as commercial enterprises, and as a result the contracts underlying them are treated as commercial-in-confidence agreements.

The main purpose of Confucius Institutes is to offer Chinese language education and associated cultural programs. University-based Confucius Institutes in Australia typically do not teach for-credit classes to ordinary university students, although some Confucius Institutes abroad do. The University of Queensland controversially allowed its Confucius Institute to partner in sponsoring several social science classes, although the details are murky.[98] It particularly came under fire for questionable China-related content in an undergraduate economics class.[99] But the mainstay of Australia's university-based Confucius Institutes is teaching Chinese language and culture courses to members of the wider community. This raises the question of why they should be based at universities at all. Other countries' community language education outreach programs tend not to be university-based, but China seems to have a strong preference for working from within established host institutions.

Australia has a higher concentration of university-based Confucius Institutes than any country besides New Zealand. They exist at Adelaide, CDU, Griffith, La Trobe, Melbourne, Newcastle, Queensland, QUT, RMIT, Sydney, UNSW, UWA, and Victoria, although the RMIT institute will reportedly close in 2021.[100] All of these except Adelaide have released their Confucius Institute agreements to the press, but in any case these agreements do not include financial details beyond the provision of a start-up grant of $150,000.[101] It is known that in a typical American Confucius Institute contract, the host university provides the physical facilities (office and classroom space) and pays for a director, while the Chinese partners provide a start-up grant on the order of USD 150,000, an annual subsidy on the order of USD 100,000, a Chinese associate director, teaching staff, books, and materials.[102] The premium-level 'model' Confucius Institute at the University of Auckland reportedly received NZD 992,571 in Chinese funding in 2017, although half of this apparently went to staffing, which seems to be considered as an in-kind contribution at most other Confucius Institutes.[103]

These are not small sums, but they are not transformative. Indeed, it is not clear that Confucius Institutes actually turn a profit at all. The RMIT Confucius Institute is reportedly being closed "due to the financial impacts of COVID-19", which strongly suggests that it is not a profit centre for the university.[104] Back-of-the-envelope calculations for other Confucius Institutes based on the number of courses they offer and the tuition levels they charge seem to suggest that few if any bring in more than a half million dollars a year, from which administrative and infrastructural expenses must be deducted. It is difficult to be any more specific than that, because it seems that not one of the hundreds of Confucius Institutes around the world publishes financial accounts. Despite an extensive search of the published research on Confucius Institutes, supplemented by consultations with some of the world's leading experts on the subject, it has proven impossible to discover any detailed accounting of Confucius Institute finances anywhere in the world.

Thus if the government decides to use its newfound powers to close Australia's Confucius Institutes, it might, strangely, be doing the universities a favour. It seems likely that hosting a Confucius Institute is a gesture that universities make to keep in China's favour, not the bonanza to university finances that many critics suspect. If hosting Confucius Institutes is as much a drag on universities' finances as it is on universities' reputations, then vice chancellors might confidentially welcome government action to close them. That would release the universities from their continuing obligations while allowing them to avoid taking responsibility for the closures. Their standing with the Chinese government might, perhaps, be undiminished. Were universities to protest the closures, it might even be enhanced.

But if not for the money, why do so many Australian universities host Confucius Institutes? They pose high reputational risks. They impose onerous administrative burdens, including the requirement that universities support visa applications for seconded Chinese staff members. They do not produce research. And they do not contribute to the universities' Chinese language offerings for their own students. Hosting a Confucius Institute does, however, create intangible goodwill for a university that wants to maintain "a sound and strategic positioning in China". Contrary to popular perceptions, that goodwill is not primarily redeemed in international student tuition dollars: there seems to be no evidence that the Chinese government steers prospective students toward particular foreign universities. The coin of Chinese goodwill is spent not on recruitment, but on research.

The structure of Australia-China research collaboration

As Australia's march up the international university rankings demonstrates, research success is the key metric on which universities are judged—and judge themselves. And Australian universities rely on China for high-citation research even more than for international students. This is especially true in the 'big science' disciplines that are central to international rankings success. Detailed research published by ACRI reveals that "in certain subject areas, Australia's collaboration with China has become vital to knowledge creation".[105] According to ACRI, collaborations with China-based researchers account for more than a quarter of all of Australia's highly-cited research publications in 13 out of the 21 broad fields indexed by Clarivate.[106] In seven fields, Australia's reliance on collaborations with Chinese universities for highly-cited publications exceeds 50%: mathematics (81.3%), materials science (77.8%), chemistry (76.2%), engineering (70.0%), computer science (64.7%), physics (60.0%), and agriculture (52.9%).

In short, without Chinese collaboration, Australian universities could not have achieved their current high standing in the international research rankings. Across all 21 fields indexed by Clarivate (including cross-field research), China collaborations account for an average of 39.1% of all of Australia's highly-cited research publications, calculated on a field-wise basis. These and the figures cited above pertain to research publications in the top 1% by citation count in each field. Additional ACRI research confirms that it is precisely for these premium, high-citation publications that Australia depends most on collaboration with China. Using the more comprehensive Elsevier Scopus database to chart the prevalence of Australia-China collaboration on research publications of all quality levels across 28 broad fields, the field-wise average level of collaboration with China drops to only 15.5% of these less-selective publications.[107]

Were the Commonwealth to take the extreme step of using its AFRA powers to halt all collaboration with Chinese universities, Australian universities would almost certainly suffer a catastrophic decline in their international rankings. By the same token, any Chinese decision to halt collaboration with Australia would have the same effect. The impact would be felt most keenly in the hard science fields that are disproportionately represented in the international rankings, and would be focused on the highly-cited research that has the greatest potential to move the rankings. By contrast, Australia's dependence on China for research collaboration is relatively low in commerce, the health sciences, the social sciences, and (in the Scopus data) the humanities. Collectively, these fields enrol by far the majority of Australian university students, but (with the exception of medicine) they are not well-represented in the international research rankings.

Thus in the broad-brush political economy of the Australian university system (and leaving medicine to one side), student fees and Commonwealth grants tied to student enrolments tend to support research and scholarship in areas with low rankings impact, while collaboration with Chinese universities is crucial to research success in areas with high rankings impact. Medicine is a special case, since it has long been treated as a national priority area, and both teaching and research in all of the health sciences are heavily subsidized by Commonwealth grants. For much of the rest of Australia's scientific establishment, access to Chinese collaboration has become indispensable. Twenty years ago, Australia had a respectable presence in international science rankings, but it was not a global scientific research powerhouse. It ranked tenth in HCRs, lagging far behind the US, UK, Canada, Germany, and Japan in numbers of HCRs per university.[108] Cooperation with China propelled Australia into the top tier.

The exact mechanism through which it has done so, however, is poorly reflected in the available statistics. Data on international collaboration are derived from the university affiliations of the authors listed on academic journal articles. The actual nationalities of the authors themselves are unknown. To find out, it would take a major biographical research effort mapping the individual career trajectories of Australia-based scientists, and even then, citizenship status could only be surmised. In any case, leading universities are highly globalised, and for most of them it is a matter of principle to recruit the best talent on a competitive basis from anywhere in the world. It would be a grave transgression of university principles to differentiate among researchers based on their nationalities or national origins. To do so would violate university non-discrimination policies and, in all likelihood, the Racial Discrimination Act.

That is right and proper, and not to be undermined in a liberal democratic country like Australia. But in a world where other countries do discriminate on the basis of nationality and national origin, it has the potential to generate perverse structural outcomes. A minor example of this can be seen in the small number of US government research grants that are available to US citizens anywhere in the world: the small subset of Australian academics who happen to be US citizens have differential access to these grants, and thus may enjoy special structural advantages vis-à-vis their non-American colleagues. In the case of the United States, a country with similar institutions to Australia (and a similar commitment to nondiscrimination), the risks posed by differential access to grants and collaboration, although structural, are not systemic. Australian universities are not meaningfully compromised by the need to retain access to the small number of citizen-restricted US government grant programs.

When it comes to China, the situation is very different. The Chinese government bestows benefits not only on Chinese citizens abroad, but also on former citizens of Chinese birth (whose acquisition of foreign citizenship it generally does not recognise), and in some cases even on non-citizens merely of Chinese descent. China's discriminatory practices are not always positive for those affected: China has been known to impose arbitrary penalties on non-citizens of Chinese birth or descent, too. Officially, it is incumbent on Australian universities and the Australian government to overlook the benefits and protest the impositions. Again: this is right and proper. But Australia's official non-discrimination does not obviate the structural effects of China's official discrimination. And, unlike American official discrimination, China's official discrimination is so extensive and pervasive that it does pose systemic risks to the Australian university system.

Although unacknowledged in studies of Australia-China research collaboration, the fact is that most of it involves collaboration between China-born academics who work at Australian universities and their colleagues in China. Prima facie, there is nothing wrong with this. Scratch the surface, and serious problems come to light. Australia is almost certainly the beneficiary of a massive academic 'brain drain' from China, with top Chinese scientists receiving offers to relocate to Australian universities—while retaining ties to their old institutions and networks in China. Thus what appears in the statistics as Australia-China research collaboration often consists of nothing more than Chinese research, conducted in China, in which one of the members of the research team has relocated to Australia. This portrayal is difficult to prove conclusively, but obvious to anyone who takes a moment to make a cursory search of the backgrounds of the collaborators involved.

Again, it must be stressed: this implies no misbehaviour on the part of the scientists involved and no malpractice on the part of their universities. But it creates structural risks all the same. The presence of a large number of China-born academics at Australian universities who depend primarily on Chinese networks for the resources to conduct their research generates strong incentives for Australian universities to acquiesce in Chinese practices and comply with Chinese demands. Government attention has naturally focused on the potential security threats posed by Chinese scientists working on strategically sensitive research in Australia.[109] These fears, ironically, get the risks backward because they wrongly assume that Chinese scientists in Australia are embedded in Australian research networks, when the reality is that they are much more likely to be embedded in Chinese ones. The real risk isn't that China will steal Australian science. It's that Australian universities will compromise their values in order to retain access to Chinese science.

China's Thousand Talents programs

Nothing better illustrates the risks embedded in Australia-China research collaboration than the participation of Australian university researchers in China's Thousand Talents programs. The 'Thousand Talents' branding was launched in 2008 and officially retired in 2018 in the wake of negative publicity and US government investigations, but it still serves as a shorthand for China's foreign recruitment efforts. Currently operating under the official label National High-End Foreign Experts Recruitment Plan, the Thousand Talents programs are a series of recruitment drives intended to bring foreign expertise to China. Although many non-Chinese academics have been involved in Thousand Talents recruitment, the main focus of these programs is on China-born academics working abroad. Thousand Talents recruitment focuses on high-achievement academic researchers in the hard sciences, but various programs also target social scientists, private sector engineers, and others. By 2017, China claimed to have recruited "more than 70 ... Nobel Prize laureates or academicians" through these programs.[110]

Of course, many countries operate international talent recruitment programs, including Australia. What's distinctive about China's Thousand Talents programs is that they encourage their recruits to remain in their overseas jobs. Instead of moving to China to take up full-time positions contributing to their new institutions, Thousand Talents awardees typically keep their day jobs at Western universities while moonlighting at Chinese partner institutions. This suits tenured academics quite well, since few are willing to give up secure, permanent, prestigious positions at Western universities for risky and potentially politicised appointments in China. Thus the typical Thousand Talents recruit may hold a prestigious professorial chair at a Western university while simultaneously heading a research centre in China, directing the work of dozens (or even hundreds) of junior academics, postdoctoral fellows, PhD students, and lab technicians whose salaries are paid by a Chinese partner university.

In one especially prominent case of Thousand Talents recruitment gone wrong, a Harvard University nano-scientist (who was not of Chinese origin) was charged by the US Department of Justice with failing to make required disclosures of foreign conflicts of interest on his US government grant applications.[111] Signing up as a 'Strategic Scientist' at the Wuhan University of Technology in 2012, he was paid USD 50,000 per month, given a lavish living allowance, and awarded "more than [US] $1.5 million to establish a research lab" in China. How many Chinese staff served under him is not known, although his contract apparently specified that he would mentor "young teachers and PhD students". He may or may not have informed his superiors at Harvard about his second job, but either way, it was revealed in the FBI's affidavit that Harvard eventually became aware of his China connections. Part of his role under his Thousand Talents agreement was to serve as director of the 'Harvard-WUT Nano Key Lab', and in early 2015 Harvard objected to his unlicensed use of the university name. The university did not, however, force him to give up his Thousand Talents position.

Although the spectacular arrest and indictment of a Harvard professor for making false claims on grant applications is truly exceptional, his participation in a Thousand Talents program with at least the passive acquiescence of university administrators is not. Many top scientists accept these appointments, and among top Western scientists of Chinese origin it is almost routine.

Whether motivated by ambition, patriotism, or the simple desire to give something back to their country of birth, many China-born scientists working abroad are eager to establish collaborations with universities and institutes in China. And again it must be stressed: there is nothing at all improper about these personal motivations. In all probability, most of the scholars involved disclose their partnerships to their Western host universities and declare their outside interests, when required, on government grant applications.

Examined at an individual level, it is entirely appropriate, even praise-worthy, that China-born scientists should help build China's research capacity. A major moral criticism of immigration policy in countries like Australia is that it deprives developing countries of their best and brightest, with countries like China bearing the costs of training young scholars only to see them emigrate once they reach maturity. When China-born scientists participate in Thousand Talents programs, it helps compensate China for this brain drain, giving emigrants the opportunity to educate new generations of young Chinese scholars back home. In this individual-level calculus, many China-born Thousand Talents scholars are actually doing a service to Western countries like Australia and the United States by repaying the moral debt that Western countries owe to China for encouraging so many of China's most talented and productive citizens to emigrate. There is, quite simply, nothing wrong with China-born scientists (who may still be Chinese citizens) doing their patriotic duty by contributing to the development of China's research infrastructure.

The moral corruption creeps in at the institutional level. Savvy Australian universities understand that their research success in fields like mathematics, materials science, and chemistry depends on maintaining their professors' access to

Thousand Talents programs. Australian universities' well-publicised focus on China research collaboration at the vice chancellor level should leave no doubt that university leaders are aware of this dependence. Considering that the University of Queensland wrote right into its vice chancellor's key performance indicators the understanding that China was "becoming the predominant provider of research globally" (note: 'provider', not 'consumer'), it is clear that at least some members of the University of Queensland senate understood that Australian universities depend on China for research collaboration, not the other way around. And that dependence demands that Australian universities keep the Chinese government onside—or risk losing their access to the massive Chinese subsidies embodied in Thousand Talents research.

When *The Australian* broke the news that dozens of Australian university academics had been recruited to participate in China's Thousand Talents programs, it headlined the reports "How the CCP Recruits Our Best and Brightest".[112] A quick glance of the biographies of most of the scientists identified makes abundantly clear that a more accurate title would have been "How Australia Recruits China's Best and Brightest". The newspaper's follow-up report was headed "China Exploits Australia's Lax Laws to Sign Up Researchers for Secretive Program".[113] Yet the Thousand Talents program, while previously little known outside academic circles, was never secret. It openly advertised in trade journals for a decade before going quiet in 2018, going so far as to hold annual open competitions for spaces. Even today, foreign academics can ask to participate in Thousand Talents programs via a well-publicised online application process.

Australian parliamentary hearings on the Thousand Talents programs focused on the possibility that Commonwealth-funded research may have benefitted Chinese universities. Australia's parliamentarians seemed not to realize that the flow of research article credits from China to Australia under these programs dwarfed any possible funding leakage in the opposite direction. The Australian Strategic Policy Institute (ASPI) claims that China "uses talent-recruitment programs to gain technology from abroad through illegal or non-transparent means", and no doubt this is technically correct if the Thousand Talents programs are lumped in with wider and sometimes related incidents of economic and military espionage.[114] But although China's Thousand Talents recruitment efforts may not be as transparent as Australian government fellowship competitions, they are far more transparent than Australian university elite recruitment programs. And they have absolutely no obligation to recruit in conformity with Australian law.

The burden of compliance for Australian university participation in Thousand Talents programs rests on the Australian universities and their professors, not on the Chinese government. Before the explosion of political interest in these programs, Australian universities seem to have chosen not to systematically track their academics' participation in them, but that can hardly be blamed on China.[115] Nor can it be blamed on their own ignorance: any research administrator who was unaware of Thousand Talents recruitment deserves to have been fired for not even bothering to read industry trade journals. In any case, despite the massive attention directed to the Thousand Talents programs in late 2020, the drafters of the AFRA decided not to require disclosure of these programs, since they represent agreements between individual Australian professors and Chinese institutions. The Australian employers of Thousand Talents scholars—that is to say, the main beneficiaries of these arrangements—are not, formally speaking, parties to the agreements.

The University Foreign Interference Taskforce convened by the education minister in August 2019 did not recognise any threat from Chinese talent recruitment programs in its published guidelines.[116] That may be because the universities themselves benefit immensely from these programs. It has been reported that at least 325 academics working for Australian institutions have received funding from China's Thousand Talents and related programs, and possibly over 600.[117] Nearly all of these are highly-cited scientists, and thus this number might be read in light of the fact that Australia hosts a total of only 305 Clarivate HCRs. By heavily subsidising the research productivity of these hundreds of Australia-based academics, the Chinese government plays a major role in boosting the research rankings of Australian universities. This is a boat that any Australian vice chancellor would be very reluctant to rock.

* * *

Have Australia's universities been corrupted by China? Australian universities' codependent research relationships with China create strong incentives for them to prioritise the preservation of Chinese goodwill over reasonable expectations for propriety and due diligence. As embarrassing as it may be to have their trade body representatives offer up non-answers to parliamentary questions about their employees' external obligations to Chinese universities, the status quo of intentional official ignorance serves their interests well. Most universities now have outside earnings policies, but Thousand Talents arrangements may not even trigger these policies, if they involve only reimbursement for travel expenses and the provision of research facilities. Where salaries are paid, they are paid offshore, in Chinese currency to Chinese bank accounts, and are essentially untraceable. Moreover, as with the Harvard professor who got in trouble with the FBI, the only transgression in these cases is usually the failure to report the income—and in Australia, this is only a violation of university policies, not a criminal offence.

The real risk posed by Thousand Talents programs isn't that Australian researchers will spy for China, or that Commonwealth research funds will be siphoned off to Chinese universities. It is that Australian universities will be morally corrupted by the lure of Chinese top-up funding for their most productive researchers. This corruption is facilitated by the fact that Australian universities are not legally parties to their professors' Thousand Talents agreements. The fact that China's Thousand Talents programs actually subsidise Australian universities is implicitly admitted by ASPI when it recommends that one strategy the Commonwealth could use to counter them is to "increase funding for the university sector and priority research areas, such as artificial intelligence, quantum science and energy storage".[118] That is tantamount to recommending that Australia should replace Chinese subsidies with domestic grants. In any case, what would prevent professors from taking both?

Even ASPI does not go so far as to recommend that universities prohibit their scientists from participating in Thousand Talents programs (though it does recommend that Australian government employees be barred). It does recommend mandatory disclosure. But whatever disclosure requirements might be placed on universities (and none have been placed so far), absent a blanket prohibition, universities will continue to face the seemingly irresistible temptation to benefit from these indirect Chinese research subsidies. And why shouldn't they? Participation in Thousand Talents programs is not necessarily a bad thing, and although universities should be open about their employees' Thousand Talents links, there seems little reason to discourage them. The real problem isn't the Thousand Talents programs themselves. It lies much closer to home.

The primary moral threat posed by Thousand Talents and related programs is that Australian universities have become so addicted to Chinese subsidies that they compromise their principles for fear of offending China. Like Chinese student fee income on the education side, Chinese government research support has gone from being a welcome extra fillip to being a core element of Australian universities' operational models. It has become so important that it warrants special attention in vice chancellors' performance indicators. The high international rankings of Australian universities, particularly Go8 universities, are so contingent on indirect Chinese research subsidies that many universities now go to great lengths to avoid alienating the Chinese government. This has nothing to do with national security. It has much more to do with national values.

Australian universities' attentiveness to the feelings of the Chinese government has been demonstrated in a series of minor, but telling, public incidents. As far back as 2013, when the University of Sydney invited the Dalai Lama to speak on campus (a 'get' that would once have been considered a major coup), sensitivity to Chinese government disapprobation has been on full display at Australian universities. Sydney first prohibited the display of university branding at the event, then moved the event off campus, and finally (under immense public scrutiny) moved the event back on campus, but in a limited venue without public access. Although no credible rationale for these repeated backflips was ever offered by the university, appearances by the Tibetan spiritual leader are widely known to provoke stern Chinese disapproval. In a farcical replay, though on a smaller scale, UNSW in 2020 deleted social media posts promoting an article on its website that highlighted criticisms of China's human rights record, then temporarily deleted the article itself, then reinstated the article amidst a barrage of criticism—but placed it on a less prominent webpage. Much more seriously, the University of Queensland in 2021 faced parliamentary scrutiny after it expelled a student in connection with incidents arising from his protests against Chinese government repression in Hong Kong.

Such incidents are only the tip of the iceberg, representing many more potential incidents that never occur because universities have learned to carefully self-censor China-sensitive content before it has the chance to appear. They are amateur mistakes. On their face, they almost make it seem as if the China-linked suppression of intellectual freedom at Australian universities is very rare: three minor incidents occurring over the course of a decade hardly make for an alarming trend. And it is true that these three incidents are 'the' three incidents that are repeatedly trotted out as evidence of university acquiescence to Chinese government pressure.[119] But, ironically, the most damning evidence is the absence of evidence: despite the fact that the Chinese government regularly (and very publicly) expresses its displeasure over even the smallest of perceived slights, only three such incidents have come to light at Australian universities over the course of a decade or more. The very scarcity of such incidents suggests that a staggering level of continuous behavioural self-regulation is going on behind the scenes.

Efforts to eliminate undue Chinese influence over Australian universities by requiring the universities to disclose their China links are doomed to fail. Even a more robust disclosure mechanism than that provided by the AFRA would do little to reshape university behaviour, since the relationships that would be disclosed are not, of themselves, embarrassing or inappropriate. Nor would the closure of university-based Confucius Institutes or the cancellation of other formal agreements do anything to change university behaviour—or the incentives that shape it. If Australian governments (Commonwealth and state) want to ensure that Australian public universities are not corrupted by Chinese influence, they should appoint serving politicians as their representatives on university senates, require that these politicians serve on executive compensation committees, and publish the performance indicators against which the performance of university executives is evaluated. A tautology it may be, but public accountability is the key to keeping universities accountable to the public.

China hasn't gained influence over Australian universities through its student flows, its Confucius Institutes, or even its research subsidies. It has gained influence through the lack of public accountability of Australian university leaders. Australian universities receive far more funding from the Australian government than they could ever hope to receive from China. But however much they may protest Commonwealth 'underfunding' and chafe at ministerial interventions in grant decisions, Australian universities know full well that their baseline Australian government funding is never at risk. Australian governments have long accepted the unequal division of labour under which the taxpayer writes the checks and the universities cash them, subject to only the broadest arms-length oversight. The Chinese government, by contrast, embraces no such principles of university autonomy, and demands full accountability for the limited support it provides to Australian universities. The battle for the soul of Australian public universities is a tug-of-war of accountability, and unless Australian governments start pulling their weight, China will win.

CHAPTER 6

Why are teaching and learning such low priorities?

The rankings obsession of Australian university vice chancellors is legendary. There are four major international ranking systems that are regularly featured on universities' websites—at least, when universities do well. And there are so many niche rankings that almost every university can find something to crow about. In addition to the four major systems, there are a plethora of niche rankings that can also be targeted. The University of Sydney, for example, ranks fourth in the world on the QS Graduate Employability Rankings, beating out Harvard (#5), Cambridge (#8), Oxford (#10), and even Melbourne (#7). Sydney also ranks second in the world on the THE Impact Rankings 2021, losing out to Manchester by a nose; RMIT and La Trobe round out the top four. In the THE Young University Rankings, UTS takes ninth place in the world; Wollongong ranks fourteenth in the QS Top 50 Under 50.

But one metric that Australian universities rarely discuss is student satisfaction—and with good reason. Since 2011, the Quality Indicators for Learning and Teaching (QILT) survey has asked Australian undergraduate students to rate the overall quality of their educational experiences, and the results are ... discouraging. The proportion of students rating their experiences as 'good' or 'excellent' has never risen above

80%. In 2010, the highest-rated public university was Deakin, at 83.5% (though the private University of Notre Dame scored 88.0% in 2019). In 2020 scores cratered at most universities, with system-wide student satisfaction falling from 78% to 69%. It thus comes as no surprise that the QILT, conducted annually for DESE by the ANU's Social Research Centre, is largely ignored in university promotional materials. In fact, until 2016 university identities were anonymised in the QILT data, explicitly in order "to avoid creating a simplistic 'league table' of higher education institutions".[120]

There are four annual QILT surveys: the flagship Student Experience Survey (SES), the Employer Satisfaction Survey (ESS), the Graduate Outcomes Survey (GOS), and the Graduate Outcomes Survey - Longitudinal (GOS-L), which surveys graduates three years after graduation. The ESS was first conducted in 2016, while the SES added an extra module in 2020 focused on the experiences of international students. Until 2020, Australian universities overall had mediocre but consistent undergraduate student satisfaction levels, with system-wide satisfaction bouncing between 78% and 80% over the period 2012-2019.[121] This was consistently lower than in the United States, Canada, or the United Kingdom, though to be fair, satisfaction scores are not necessarily comparable across countries.[122] Time series figures for undergraduate and postgraduate coursework student satisfaction from the SES are plotted in Figure 7, along with employer satisfaction scores from the ESS.

These averages reported in Figure 7 cover students at Bond, Divinity, and Torrens in addition to those attending Table A universities. The sharp 2020 decline in undergraduate student satisfaction is hardly surprising, under the circumstances. A similar through less precipitous decline occurred in postgraduate

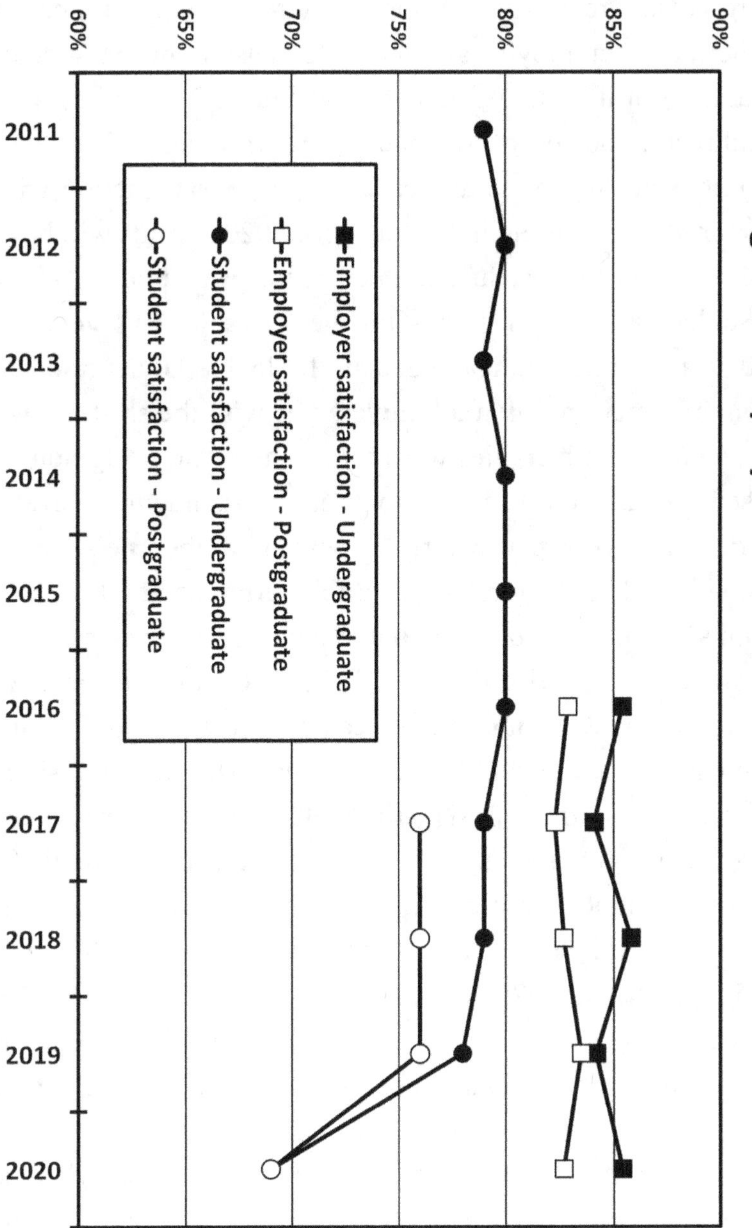

Figure 7. Employer and student satisfaction levels

coursework student satisfaction. Interestingly, headline employer satisfaction remained high, and even increased for undergraduate recruits. But these figures actually represent whether or not employers are likely "to consider hiring another graduate from the same course and institution", which is only an indirect indicator of satisfaction.[123] After all, what other institutions are there? In any case, employer satisfaction with new recruits is a lagging indicator, since 2020 recruits will have received most of their education before the pandemic.

Student satisfaction scores for the 38 Table A universities in 2019 and 2020 are compared in Table 12. Undergraduate student satisfaction fell at all universities with the shift online, although a few universities were able to maintain postgraduate coursework student satisfaction at pre-pandemic levels. The declines were particularly severe at Melbourne's major universities. The University of Melbourne itself—by most accounts, Australia's top-ranked university—barely cleared the 50% student satisfaction threshold in 2020. Granted, the sudden switch to online teaching in 2020 caught universities off-guard all across the world, but some teaching-focused universities rode out the storm surprisingly well. Australia's research-focused Go8 universities, by contrast, performed particularly poorly. Highlighted in grey in Table 12, their average student satisfaction levels fell from an already-low 76.5% in 2019 to a troubling 63.5% in 2020.

The QILT survey shows a small negative correlation between university size and undergraduate student satisfaction (r = -.252 for 2019). Australian universities have grown dramatically in size over the last two decades, whether measured in terms of revenue or of student numbers. Most of them are now very large by international standards, with some Go8 universities ranking among the largest in the world.[124]

Table 12. Student satisfaction with educational experience (%)

University	Undergraduate			Postgraduate		
	2019	2020	Change	2019	2020	Change
ACU	79.4	71.0	-8.4	66.6	68.9	2.3
Adelaide	79.0	69.7	-9.3	73.8	63.6	-10.2
ANU	79.6	67.9	-11.7	72.7	63.8	-8.9
Canberra	78.3	69.0	-9.3	75.3	72.4	-2.9
CDU	75.2	68.5	-6.7	67.8	60.2	-7.6
CQU	77.5	75.3	-2.2	75.8	71.6	-4.2
CSU	77.3	70.6	-6.7	78.0	76.6	-1.4
Curtin	80.0	71.7	-8.3	79.0	72.7	-6.3
Deakin	83.5	72.9	-10.6	79.9	72.8	-7.1
ECU	83.3	81.5	-1.8	78.9	76.2	-2.7
Federation	79.6	69.2	-10.4	81.0	69.0	-12.0
Flinders	78.1	70.8	-7.3	70.9	71.6	0.7
Griffith	82.1	70.7	-11.4	82.5	75.0	-7.5
JCU	75.2	65.6	-9.6	70.0	72.3	2.3
La Trobe	75.9	66.7	-9.2	73.0	65.4	-7.6
Macquarie	78.4	70.4	-8.0	73.8	63.4	-10.4
Melbourne	77.6	52.3	-25.3	77.5	58.1	-19.4
Monash	78.6	60.4	-18.2	74.7	60.2	-14.5
Murdoch	79.8	70.8	-9.0	79.5	73.8	-5.7
Newcastle	79.2	66.4	-12.8	78.4	75.3	-3.1
Notre Dame	88.0	74.1	-13.9	81.7	77.2	-4.5
Queensland	80.0	66.3	-13.7	75.5	64.6	-10.9
QUT	81.8	65.8	-16.0	80.0	71.4	-8.6
RMIT	78.5	62.1	-16.4	75.8	63.0	-12.8
SCU	79.4	70.2	-9.2	76.9	78.4	1.5
Swinburne	80.5	72.9	-7.6	78.1	71.4	-6.7
Sydney	74.2	63.6	-10.6	73.4	58.9	-14.5
Tasmania	77.5	71.8	-5.7	69.6	63.0	-6.6
UNE	83.2	80.6	-2.6	83.1	80.9	-2.2
UNISA	79.2	73.9	-5.3	75.5	68.3	-7.2
UNSW	62.9	59.7	-3.2	72.0	65.0	-7.0
USC	81.5	73.0	-8.5	71.1	80.0	8.9
USQ	75.7	74.6	-1.1	79.2	77.6	-1.6
UTS	77.4	65.7	-11.7	76.5	64.5	-12.0
UWA	79.7	68.4	-11.3	71.1	65.0	-6.1
Victoria	75.4	69.5	-5.9	72.5	67.2	-5.3
Wollongong	81.0	66.7	-14.3	72.2	68.4	-3.8
WSU	76.2	67.1	-9.1	72.5	64.0	-8.5

Nonetheless, the notion persists among the commentariat that they are undersized, and that by growing still further they could "offer more programs, improved campuses and better academic staff".[125] The QILT results indicate that students, at least, do not perceive size as an advantage. What's more, the extreme drop in student satisfaction between 2019 and 2020 was quite strongly correlated with university size (r = -.503), with the biggest universities recording the largest declines in student satisfaction in the first year of the pandemic.

In terms of undergraduate student satisfaction, the overall picture seems to be that bigger is neither better nor particularly worse, but that bigger universities flubbed their pandemic responses. This may be because, when push came to shove, Australia's biggest universities systematically prioritized research over teaching. There is a strong overlap between research intensiveness and university size in Australia: Go8 universities are on average 50% larger than non-Go8 universities, and five of Australia's six largest universities by EFTSL are in the Go8. Anecdotal evidence strongly suggests that these large, research-intensive universities protected research-focused staff in 2020 while making substantial cuts to teaching-focused academics, especially casual teachers. This suggestion is reinforced by the fact that the Commonwealth's $1 billion bailout package was entirely dedicated to research.

Full DESE staffing figures for 2020 will not be released until 2022, but Universities Australia claims that "Australian universities shed at least 17,300 jobs in 2020".[126] More than 7500 university jobs were lost in Victoria alone.[127] These figures suggest that Australian universities made staff headcount cuts of greater than 10% from 2019 levels. Yet press reports of cuts to research-focused and teaching-and-research academic staff suggested that these job losses ran into the hundreds, not the tens of thousands.[128]

It seems clear that job cuts have primarily affected casual teaching staff, not permanent staff or casual researchers.[129] This is confirmed by the many complaints made by students during the pandemic of the tenor that "remote classes were overcrowded and impersonal, with up to six times more students in an online tutorial than a physical one before the pandemic".[130]

Given that declines in enrolment were relatively small (down 3.3% in New South Wales and approximately 3% in Victoria, according to the respective state auditors' reports), double-digit cuts in teaching staff seem wildly disproportionate. Universities Australia reports that the country's universities suffered a collective 'operating revenue' decline of 4.9% in 2020, which in real terms would have come to 5%.[131] That is indeed serious. But had all university academic staff been employed on an equal split between teaching and research, enrolment declines on the order of 3% could have been accommodated through a mix of hiring freezes, general economies, and recourse to reserves. Of course, this would have resulted in a concomitant reduction in university research output. Instead, universities seem to have maintained research staff numbers at a relatively constant level, leaving teaching to bear the full brunt of the 5% revenue decline. If this is the case, the decline in student-facing staff hours must have been large indeed.

The problem of low student engagement

One thing that certainly happened in 2020 was that all universities were forced, at short notice, to shift their default modes of instruction from in-person to online. Some private providers like Torrens were already running large-scale online operations before 2020, but most public universities were caught off-guard. Many of them—including seven of the Go8—

had built their online strategies around offering massive open online courses (MOOCs) on the two major global platforms, Coursera (Macquarie, Melbourne, Sydney, UNSW, UWA) and edX (Adelaide, ANU, Curtin, Newcastle, Queensland). These platforms do not, however, generally support the delivery of full undergraduate degrees. The much smaller FutureLearn platform has a wider membership of Australian universities, but only Newcastle uses the platform to offer a full undergraduate degree: a Bachelor of Arts cobbled together from short courses in a variety of disciplines.

Despite headlines proclaiming "exponential growth" in enrolments, MOOC growth was surprisingly lacklustre in 2020.[132] Peel off the thick layer of marketing goo, and what you find are millions of people signing up for free personal development webinars, a surge in Indian students topping up their science skills, and a big boost in MOOC registrations that seems not to have translated into paid coursework. The largest MOOC provider, Coursera, lost USD 66.8 million in 2020 on revenues of USD 293.5 in 2020.[133] Although it recorded revenue growth of 59%, Coursera is still no larger than a smallish Australian public university, enrolling only around 11,000 degree students globally, mostly at the master's level. Although many students turned to MOOCs for upskilling in 2020, none of the major platforms proved flexible enough to accommodate an emergency shift online in full-scale university degree courses.

Thus the pandemic that should have confirmed the dominance of the MOOC model instead proved its irrelevance. The standard MOOC operating model centres on the professional studio recording of unit material, with teachers delivering scripted lectures, often using a teleprompter. Self-check quizzes are preprogrammed at frequent stages, with graded homework or online exams set for paid classes. Student participation is generally managed through online bulletin boards. The model has high up-front costs, with the prospective payoff coming from economies of scale. It may ultimately work for a small number of static, standardized units of study (like basic algebra or Greek philosophy), and it seems to work for a small number of dynamic, celebrity-driven units that are updated every year (like Yale's "Science of Wellbeing" and Harvard's "Introduction to Computer Science"). But it would be prohibitively expensive for a university to attempt to put its entire slate of offerings online using the MOOC model.

Thus when Australian universities went online in April 2020, most of their existing strategies went out the window. In fact, it turned out that going online was as simple as scheduling a Zoom meeting. Notwithstanding some exceptions in specialised disciplines like medicine and social work, the bulk of student experiences at Australian universities in 2020 and 2021 consisted of Zoom classes. Unsurprisingly, the move to Zoom coincided with a precipitous decline in student satisfaction. But more detailed data available from the SES point to a more specific problem. In addition to overall student satisfaction, the SES also measures student satisfaction with four particular aspects of the educational experience: teaching quality, skills development, learning resources, and learner engagement. The first two of these held up reasonably well in 2020, while a modest decline in satisfaction with access to learning resources (like libraries and laboratories) was unavoidable. But by far the biggest coronavirus shift uncovered by the SES was a 16-point decline in satisfaction with learner engagement.

The system-wide trajectory of undergraduate student satisfaction on all four SES subscores is plotted in Figure 8. Three clear trends pop out of the chart. First, students are relatively well-satisfied with the quality of teaching, the content of teaching, and the physical facilities of Australian universities. Second, some 40% of Australian students have been dissatisfied with their opportunities for engagement throughout the 2010s. Third, an absolute majority of students were dissatisfied with their opportunities for engagement in 2020. The chronically low level of student satisfaction with learner engagement is striking: the student engagement crisis at Australian universities is not a passing problem, but a structural feature of the system. The crisis worsened in 2020, but it's been there all along, and universities have failed to address it for a decade or more.

The SES learner engagement subscale is a composite measure based on student answers to questions about their feelings of preparation, sense of belonging, participation in discussions, work with other students, interaction outside the classroom, and interaction with students from different backgrounds.[134] Results for the individual items are not reported, but the overall score doesn't leave much room for doubt about the overall message. A worryingly large proportion of Australian students simply are not satisfied with what might be called the 'social' side of the university experience. And the dissatisfaction with engagement is widespread: no Australian public university achieved higher than 70% undergraduate satisfaction with learner engagement. With the online transition of 2020, no public university broke above 53%. The SES learner engagement satisfaction rates (undergraduate and postgraduate coursework) for all 39 Table A universities are reported in Table 13.

Why were satisfaction levels so low before the coronavirus-induced move to Zoom? Few people seem to realise it, but Australian universities have been mostly online for a decade or more. Even before the coronavirus crisis, it was standard practice for classes to be recorded using automated classroom recording systems, and nearly all assignments were submitted

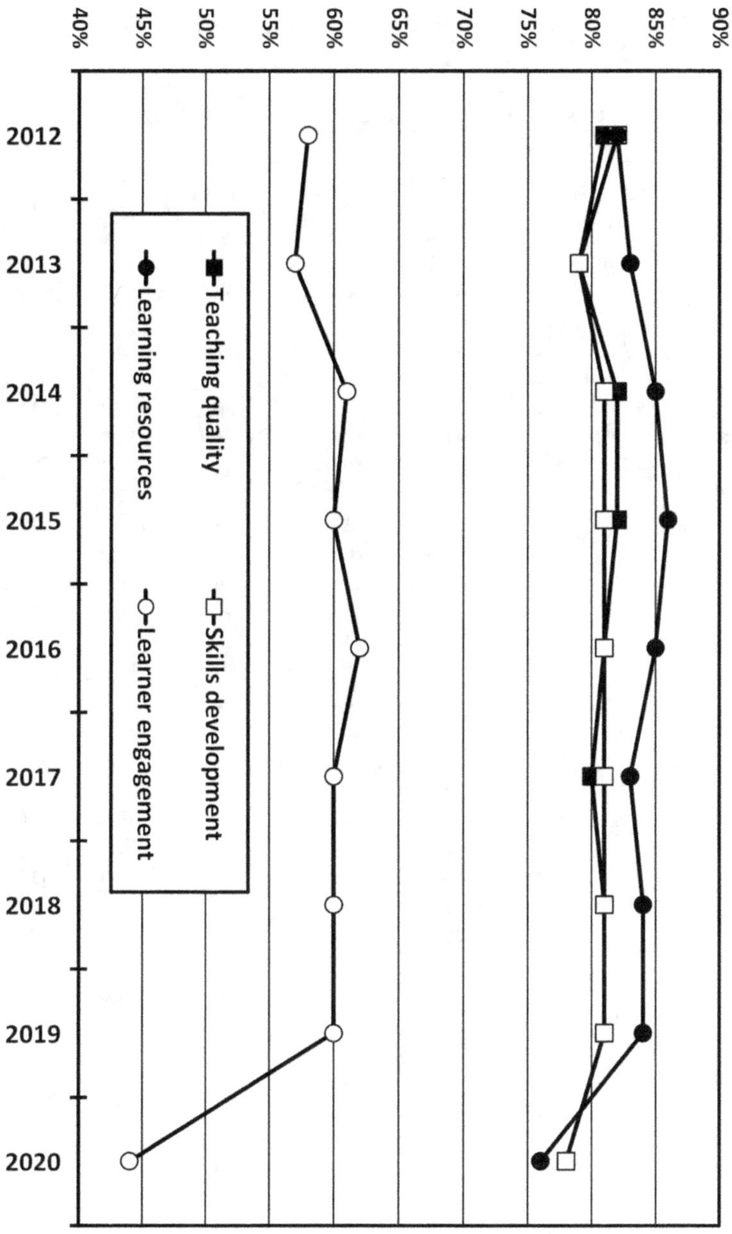

Figure 8. Undergraduate student satisfaction detail

Table 13. Student satisfaction with learner engagement (%)

University	Undergraduate			Postgraduate		
	2019	2020	Change	2019	2020	Change
ACU	67.0	53.0	-14.0	48.7	38.3	-10.4
Adelaide	64.3	49.5	-14.8	54.7	47.8	-6.9
ANU	59.1	43.2	-15.9	53.5	41.1	-12.4
Canberra	59.1	50.0	-9.1	62.4	56.1	-6.3
CDU	47.8	30.1	-17.7	61.3	39.1	-22.2
CQU	47.4	30.7	-16.7	62.6	54.3	-8.3
CSU	63.4	33.5	-29.9	55.3	30.9	-24.4
Curtin	66.5	46.8	-19.7	67.1	40.0	-27.1
Deakin	61.6	37.9	-23.7	64.9	37.2	-27.7
ECU	66.5	54.6	-11.9	66.8	52.2	-14.6
Federation	65.9	47.9	-18.0	64.1	56.0	-8.1
Flinders	64.5	53.6	-10.9	61.2	39.2	-22.0
Griffith	64.4	42.6	-21.8	69.3	39.9	-29.4
JCU	64.5	50.6	-13.9	62.1	33.4	-28.7
La Trobe	65.3	44.5	-20.8	58.4	42.8	-15.6
Macquarie	57.1	41.5	-15.6	59.7	39.9	-19.8
Melbourne	58.5	34.0	-24.5	61.3	38.6	-22.7
Monash	66.4	32.4	-34.0	56.1	30.9	-25.2
Murdoch	55.8	46.1	-9.7	67.9	58.9	-9.0
Newcastle	59.9	41.8	-18.1	62.3	33.2	-29.1
Notre Dame	77.3	61.6	-15.7	59.2	60.5	1.3
Queensland	63.2	44.1	-19.1	62.0	41.9	-20.1
QUT	65.8	44.8	-21.0	65.0	41.0	-24.0
RMIT	66.5	46.0	-20.5	63.4	38.8	-24.6
SCU	59.4	30.5	-28.9	56.5	23.2	-33.3
Swinburne	65.4	40.9	-24.5	66.0	46.4	-19.6
Sydney	57.8	41.9	-15.9	58.0	40.9	-17.1
Tasmania	61.2	29.6	-31.6	62.4	35.3	-27.1
UNE	66.0	21.9	-44.1	62.7	18.6	-44.1
UNISA	63.8	49.7	-14.1	66.7	51.0	-15.7
UNSW	56.0	42.2	-13.8	49.9	33.8	-16.1
USC	61.7	46.7	-15.0	59.6	60.0	0.4
USQ	51.9	31.2	-20.7	62.4	28.8	-33.6
UTS	68.4	46.9	-21.5	64.7	48.6	-16.1
UWA	58.5	53.0	-5.5	70.5	57.1	-13.4
Victoria	68.5	61.2	-7.3	68.6	51.6	-17.0
Wollongong	69.3	42.6	-26.7	64.5	46.9	-17.6
WSU	62.4	48.2	-14.2	61.1	42.7	-18.4

electronically. Australian universities do not publish attendance statistics, but it is likely that the majority of Australian students in high-enrolment disciplines like the humanities, the social sciences, science, and business were effectively attending online (by watching lecture recordings) even before 2020—if they were attending at all. Anecdotal reports suggest that attendance rates are abysmal, with one broad-based study reporting a figure of 38%.[135] Although low attendance is often blamed on lecture recordings, at least one study conducted in 2007 reported similarly low levels—and that, at a law school.[136]

The shift to all-online instruction in 2020 thus didn't so much undermine Australia's system of university education as reinforce it. Even before the partial online transition of the 2010s, student engagement was already low. The Australian grading system, in which a bare 'pass' is a socially acceptable (if not exactly praiseworthy) mark, and in which most students are relegated by design to receiving 'pass' or 'credit' results, certainly does little to promote attendance. As the popular student aphorism has it, "the P gets the degree". This lackadaisical attitude encourages a "we pretend to teach / you pretend to learn" compact between teachers and students in which both can get away with a bare minimum effort. The most straightforward reading of the available data is that most Australian university students are able to pass their classes without actually attending class. This further suggests that most classes don't really add much value.

To be clear, this is not what students are complaining about. Their beef is with the lack of engagement, not with the quality of instruction. But it's not very meaningful to say that students are satisfied with their teachers and the skills they learn in class, when they don't attend so much as half the classes they are supposedly evaluating. A skeptical, perhaps cynical, interpretation would be that students aren't learning much in class, and are happy not to have to learn much. Nor do high employer satisfaction levels contradict this interpretation. Most of the items on the ESS evaluate vague professional skills like "ability to solve problems", "ability to identify new opportunities", "getting on well with others", "using technology effectively", and "ability to work under pressure".[137] The ESS does not ask employers how well graduates understand, say, actuarial tables or circuit design.

This is not to say that Australian undergraduate students spend three or four years doing nothing at all. But it does seem that Australian students are less connected to their universities than would be ideal, and much less connected than the taxpayers who subsidise their tuition might like. There is no obvious reason why attendance rates should be allowed to plummet from more than 90% to less than 50% with the transition from high school to university, unless it really is true that most university classes teach nothing important. If that is the case, why should the taxpayer subsidise them? Low student engagement is the canary in the coal mine for assessing educational quality. The solution isn't to find ways for students to make friends and feel engaged outside of class. It's to get students to class, where they will make friends, and hopefully engage with class material while they are there.

The proliferation of courses

Many of the questions included in the SES ask students to evaluate the courses in which they are enrolled. As a reminder, a course is a "coherent sequence of units of study leading to an award of a qualification" that may or may not be a degree.[138] Universities typically offer courses that lead to bachelor and master degrees, but sometimes these courses are embedded in larger degree programs. For example, graduate certificates (typically requiring 6 months of full-time study) and graduate diplomas (12 months) are often embedded within master degrees (18-24 months), meaning that students can in theory complete both graduate certificate and graduate diploma qualifications on the way to finishing a master degree. Similarly, diplomas, associate degrees, and honours degrees can be embedded in bachelor degree courses.

It would be interesting to see student satisfaction statistics broken out by course: interesting, but not very practical. Australian higher education providers collectively offer more than 25,000 distinct courses, or roughly one course for every 64 students. The exact number of courses being offered in Australia is unknown, both because it is always changing and because course data for self-accrediting institutions (like public universities) are not available from TEQSA. Data are, however, available for courses that are registered with DESE to be offered onshore to international students. The Commonwealth Register of Institutions and Courses for Overseas Students (CRICOS) exists to serve as the basis for the issuing of student visas, but it can serve as a proxy for the courses available to domestic students as well. The 25,279 active courses listed in CRICOS as of June 30, 2021 represent a lower bound on the total number of courses offered in Australia, since some domestic-only courses might not be included, but practically speaking the CRICOS list is likely to be comprehensive.

The CRICOS database is also a rich source of trivia on Australian higher education. The longest and most expensive bachelor course offered by an Australian university is Sydney's Bachelor of Medical Science / Bachelor of Medicine / Bachelor of Surgery, which requires a full seven years of study at an estimated cost of $536,591. Forty-one courses include mandatory industry placement work components that exceed 40 hours per week, led by Griffith's MD course, which apparently requires students to work 121 hours per week (more than 17 hours a day) for 20 weeks straight. And considering Australia's high immigrant population and extraordinary number of international students, surprisingly few providers teach courses in languages other than English. Various religious institutions teach 7 courses in Chinese and 12 in Korean, a French school teaches one course in French, and UTS offers an MA and PhD in international studies taught in Chinese. That's it.

More importantly, the sheer number of courses available makes the transition from school to university potentially very confusing for Australian teenagers. The typical Australian university offers a bewildering array of more than 90 bachelor degrees, producing a combined total of 3583 bachelor degree choices. The number of bachelor and master degree courses offered by each of the 38 Table A universities is given in Table 14. Two universities stand out for the relatively small number of bachelor degree courses they offer: Melbourne (23) and UWA (28). Sixteen others offer 100 or more bachelor degree courses—and that's not counting master degree courses, of which there nearly as many (3139) as bachelor degrees. The University of Sydney takes the prize for the largest number of CRICOS-registered courses, with 820 courses of all kinds, giving an average of 84 students per course.

It would be disingenuous to make too much of this proliferation of courses; to a large extent, it simply reflects the fact that most Australian universities follow the British model of defining courses narrowly instead of the American model of defining causes broadly. The British model tends to lock young scholars into highly structured courses at a time in their lives when they may not fully understand what those courses even

Table 14. Courses offered by universities

University	Bachelor	Master	All courses
ACU	81	30	188
Adelaide	102	89	461
ANU	53	158	376
Canberra	177	48	311
CDU	67	39	202
CQU	36	20	158
CSU	57	18	122
Curtin	75	95	463
Deakin	86	68	259
ECU	97	49	240
Federation	117	43	250
Flinders	135	101	443
Griffith	124	87	366
JCU	35	28	149
La Trobe	102	95	349
Macquarie	121	218	451
Melbourne	23	228	465
Monash	161	171	597
Murdoch	83	46	233
Newcastle	72	67	454
Notre Dame	71	13	145
Queensland	99	150	424
QUT	113	40	270
RMIT	123	93	505
SCU	66	21	161
Swinburne	88	102	355
Sydney	145	283	820
Tasmania	101	82	448
UNE	48	23	139
UNISA	98	58	352
UNSW	125	119	583
USC	83	19	156
USQ	49	33	142
UTS	161	113	499
UWA	28	82	276
Victoria	62	55	282
Wollongong	158	77	412
WSU	161	78	423

are, what careers they might lead to, and indeed what careers they themselves might want to pursue in life. The American model, by contrast, is more flexible, allowing students to change majors within courses until relatively late in their undergraduate careers. The American model may produce fewer regrets than the British model, but it does so at the price that undergraduates often end up with generalist first degrees, and require further postgraduate coursework before starting their adult careers.

The American model was adopted at Melbourne in 2008 with an attempt to consolidate all its bachelor degrees into six courses, and thus it came to be known in Australia as the 'Melbourne Model'. This pioneering effort was followed by a 2012 transition at UWA from 62 bachelor degree courses to just five. Melbourne never quite got down to six degree courses, but it came close, and has only crept up since due to a fracturing of its studio arts offerings into multiple specialisations. The University of Western Australia did make it down to five bachelor degree courses, and held that line until 2020, when a new vice chancellor quietly threw in the towel. Despite traditionalist resistance, the Melbourne Model offers a positive vision for the future of undergraduate education in Australia. But as the experiences of both Melbourne and (especially) UWA demonstrate, that vision is stillborn.

At UWA, the initial suite of five undergraduate degrees really consisted of four degrees (Arts, Commerce, Design, and Science) plus a high-ATAR elite degree with embedded honours labeled the 'Bachelor of Philosophy' that allowed students to pursue a major in any of the four basic degrees. This lasted until 2018, when a high-ATAR Bachelor of Biomedical Science was carved out of the ordinary Bachelor of Science, with the Bachelor of Design being retired to compensate. But the dam was broken, and in 2021 UWA introduced six new courses and a slew of combined courses. The university will offer another 13 new bachelor courses in 2022. In its 2020 annual report, UWA offered a terse two-word explanation for the abandonment of its eight-year experiment with the Melbourne Model: 'increased competition'.[139]

In a well-regulated market for undergraduate courses, universities would compete to attract the best students by offering desirable student experiences that lead to successful student outcomes. Universities would offer a limited number of standardised degree courses, on which systematic data could be collected and league tables compiled. Relevant metrics might include average class sizes, international student enrolments, student satisfaction levels, graduation rates, graduate employment outcomes, and graduate salaries—all reported at the course level. Reinforced by anecdotal feedback from current students and graduates, these data would give prospective students the tools they need to make well-informed decisions about their university studies.

But in Australia's almost unregulated market for undergraduate courses, the pressure of competition has been shifted from course differentiation to admissions segmentation based on target Australian Tertiary Admission Rank (ATAR) levels. Innovation focuses on designing attractive-sounding degree labels that can be attached to stratified ATAR 'price' points. Star students are encouraged to pursue elite high-ATAR degrees, instead of 'wasting' their ATARs on degrees with low minimum entry cutoffs. This might make sense, if these stratified degrees segmented students into distinct disciplinary cohorts; for example, medicine versus nursing. Instead, ATAR competition, reinforced by competition for international student enrolments, has created a system in which degrees are proliferated purely for admissions marketing purposes. Students in these bespoke degrees sit side by side in the same classrooms, learning the same material, despite undertaking notionally distinct programs of study.

At the University of Sydney, for example, a student can complete a major in psychology leading to an honours year and eventual professional accreditation through any one of 18 different undergraduate courses, including the Bachelor of Liberal Arts and Sciences (with an ATAR guide rank of 70), the Bachelor of Arts (80), the Bachelor of Science (80), the Bachelor of Science and Bachelor of Advanced Studies - Advanced (90), the Bachelor of Psychology (95), and the Bachelor of Science and Bachelor of Advanced Studies - Dalyell Scholars (98). With minor exceptions, students in all of these courses will take the same 10 units of study that constitute the psychology major. The 18 different courses allow students to do different things alongside their psychology majors, and can be defended as catering to student interests. But if they existed primarily to cater to student interests, why not assign them the same minimum ATAR?

It is hard to escape the conclusion that the primary purpose of these ornate course offerings is to segment the student market by ATAR. This kind of ATAR segmentation has little to do with ensuring that students are matched with degree courses for which they are properly prepared to succeed, since students with wildly different minimum ATARs are allowed to study in literally the same classes. Access to some fields, like medicine and law, is meaningfully rationed by ATAR, and these fields are rightly designated as distinct degree courses with their own entry criteria. It also makes sense to segment access to other fields that require extensive specialised study to meet the requirements of professional certification, like education, nursing, and social work. But it is nothing short of obfuscation for universities to proliferate 'here today, gone tomorrow' bachelor degree courses that consist of little more than the reshuffling of shared units of study.

A market-based alternative

Universities have always existed to prepare young people to enter the professions. England's ancient universities at Oxford and Cambridge, and later America's first university at Cambridge, Massachusetts (Harvard University), were founded primarily to prepare students for the clergy. Back then, this was as much as to say that it prepared them for careers as clerks. The English words clergy, cleric, clerical, and clerk are all derived from the same Latin word, reflecting a time when writing and numeracy were primarily the province of the church. And it is just as true today as it was in the twelfth century that the most likely fate of a BA graduate is to undertake clerical work of some kind: i.e., paperwork. The documents involved have progressed from parchment to paper to electronic files, but BA graduates still busy themselves composing official correspondence and totting up columns of figures.

Back in the Middle Ages, when the BA was the only undergraduate degree on offer, professional courses were relegated to the postgraduate level. In the American university system, this remains the norm (despite many exceptions). In the Australian university system, by contrast, professional degrees have been offered at the undergraduate level from the very beginning, starting with law and medicine way back in the 1850s. Early specialisation has always been a feature of the Australian university system, and although the merits of early versus late specialisation have long been debated, no consensus has ever emerged in favour of changing the system. Taking for granted that Australian universities will continue to offer professional degrees at the undergraduate level, some amount of course proliferation is inevitable.

But it is not inevitable that the typical university should offer 90-odd undergraduate degree courses, many of them with overlapping content. System-wide, prospective higher education students in Australia face the bewildering prospect of choosing from among no fewer than 5044 distinct undergraduate courses, counting equivalent courses at different institutions separately. Aggregating courses across institutions still leaves prospective students 3417 different course titles to choose from, each of them leading to one, two, or (in some cases) three undergraduate degrees. The most extravagant of these, Sydney's triple-degree courses in medicine, surgery, and the student's choice of commerce, music, or science, take seven years. Wollongong's Bachelor of Engineering (Honours) - Bachelor of Laws also takes seven years, and many other universities have combined bachelor degrees that take five or more years to complete.

Outside the vapid logic of marketing, there seems no reason to retain students in undergraduate study for five, six, or even seven years. Universities, however, benefit from bundling multiple undergraduate degrees into combined courses because it helps them keep students enrolled for longer periods in Commonwealth-supported places. This educationally and financially profligate practice is made possible by the government's bizarre decision not to place limits on the number of undergraduate degrees a student can take with government support. Under current regulations, students can literally spend their whole lives in full-time undergraduate study in Commonwealth-supported places (although there are limits on how much students can borrow from the government). Universities are thus incentivised to hold onto students for as long as they can, even though it would make more pedagogical sense to encourage students to progress from undergraduate to postgraduate study.

A more student-centred, market-driven approach to structuring undergraduate courses would limit universities to offering a finite number of single-degree courses while limiting students to one lifetime undergraduate degree course on a Commonwealth-supported place. Self-accrediting higher education providers like universities might have broad latitude to customise individual courses as they see fit, but in the end they would have to structure each of their undergraduate degree courses to fit under one of a dozen or so standard labels (e.g., Bachelor of Arts, Bachelor of Science, Bachelor of Engineering, etc.) approved for funding by the government. Annual student satisfaction and employment outcome surveys like those currently undertaken by the QILT program could then report outcomes by degree for each university offering that degree course.

Under such a system, students would have the information they need to make informed decisions about their futures—and about the universities competing to attract their government-subsidised dollars. Universities, unable to compete on branding (since degree names would be standardised) or on price (for Commonwealth-supported places), would be forced to compete on outcomes. The Commonwealth would benefit from reduced costs, as students progressed logically from highly subsidised undergraduate study to less-subsidised postgraduate study. Alternatively, existing Commonwealth funding could be used to make undergraduate degree courses available for more students, instead of concentrating funds on a smaller number of students wastefully pursuing multiple degrees. With an expected increase in the number of domestic students needing university places in the 2020s, it would make a lot of sense to provide more students with one bachelor degree than fewer students with multiple degrees.

Job-ready graduates?

Under the current funding regime, the government cooperates with universities to perpetuate an opaque system that forestalls the operation of market forces and incentivises perverse behaviour on the part of both universities and students. The 2020 Job-ready Graduates Package only reinforced existing practices that make it almost impossible for prospective students to evaluate the relative merits of different degree courses. Intended to steer students toward career-relevant degrees, the Job-ready Graduates Package only obscured the (modest) price signals that had previously been embedded in student contribution amounts, substituting in their place a central planner's vision of future trends. It sorted subject areas into four funding tiers based on perceptions of future employability that are entirely divorced from existing data.

This is illustrated in Table 15, which matches the rates of full-time employment (among those seeking work) for 2019 graduates in the 21 broad subject areas covered by the GOS with the four student contribution bands from the Job-ready Graduates Package. Full-time employment rates in 2019 for 2016 graduates are also reported, based on data from the GOS-L. More recent data are available for 2020, but data for 2019 have been used in Table 15 in order to avoid potential coronavirus distortions. Under the Job-ready Graduates Package, Band 1 subjects are priced at the lowest cost to students ($3,950 on an annualised basis in 2021) and Band 4 subjects are priced the highest ($14,500).

There is no clear relationship between the employment rates and price bands shown in Table 15. The low correlation

Table 15. Graduate employability by subject (2019)

Study area	FT emp. rate	3-year rate	Job-Ready
Creative arts	52.9%	79.7%	Band 2
Tourism/hospitality	56.4%	82.4%	Band 4
Communications	60.1%	85.1%	Band 4
Math/science	63.4%	87.8%	Bands 1/2
Psychology	63.4%	84.0%	Band 1
Humanities/society	64.3%	86.2%	Band 4
Social work	70.2%	87.4%	Band 2
Health services	70.5%	90.7%	Band 2
Agriculture	72.6%	92.4%	Band 1
Architecture	74.5%	91.9%	Band 2
Computing/IT	75.9%	91.4%	Band 2
Nursing	76.3%	93.0%	Band 1
Business/commerce	76.6%	93.6%	Band 4
Law and paralegal	77.3%	95.2%	Band 4
Teacher education	80.8%	93.3%	Band 1
Veterinary science	81.9%	95.6%	Band 3
Engineering	84.8%	95.4%	Band 2
Dentistry	86.2%	98.6%	Band 3
Medicine	91.1%	98.2%	Band 3
Rehabilitation	92.4%	97.5%	Band 2
Pharmacy	95.7%	93.5%	Band 2

of $r = -0.119$ for immediate employment drops to essentially zero ($r = -0.030$) at three years. The correlations for graduate pay (not shown in Table 15) are similar. Pay at graduation is slightly lower for more expensive courses ($r = -0.091$), but this modest relationship reverses after three years ($r = 0.127$). Math and science graduates have slightly lower employment rates (at slightly lower pay) when compared to humanities and social science graduates. In short, there's 'nothing there' in the data; from a price signaling perspective, the government's student contribution bands might as well be random. In any case, it is not clear that price signaling is an effective mechanism for nudging student decision-making, in light of the fact that student contributions are financed at concessional rates by government-subsidised loan programs.

Given the profound uncertainty that always surrounds the economic future, it would make more sense for the Commonwealth either to price all degrees at the same rate or to price individual degrees in line with costs. The government could then give students the tools they need to identify the degrees that best fit with their own future plans. Moreover, if the Commonwealth were to standardise a list of single-degree courses and offer to fund only courses drawn from that list, it could much more easily calculate the cost of a course for price-setting purposes. Alternatively, it could deregulate fees and offer to pay either a fixed amount or a fixed proportion of the fees for each course. Whatever model the government selected, students would need clear outcomes data in order to make informed decisions about their degree choices. Such data can only be provided in an environment of standardised and stable undergraduate degree course offerings.

The Job-ready Graduates Package was a lost opportunity for reform, but not the last opportunity. Its goals were broadly correct: to create tens of thousands of new university places, encourage study in regional Australia, create a more integrated system of higher education, raise transparency, and improve accountability.[140] But it was poorly and clumsily designed to meet these goals, and seemingly calculated to confront universities rather than to reshape them. In promulgating the legislation, the government accepted battle on the universities' chosen terrain: funding and places. It should instead have sought to reshape the terrain. The restructuring of the undergraduate course market in ways that promote competition, comparison, and ranking would further the

Commonwealth's stated priorities while giving students the tools they need to ensure their own job-readiness. The people best placed to evaluate students' future career prospects are, after all, the students themselves.

* * *

Why are teaching and learning such low priorities? Whenever pundits, the universities, or the government discuss research, their focus is always on 'excellence'. When they talk teaching, they focus on numbers. Instead of ranking universities (and their many courses) on the basis of student outcomes, they shift the conversation over to enrolments, fees, and subsidies. Research is sexy. It offers dramatic visuals for university websites and produces a regular stream of 'findings' to fill feel-good press releases. Research is also the currency of academic prestige and vice chancellors' bragging rights. Improving student outcomes, by contrast, is plain hard work. It is a tough battle for incremental gains that starts afresh with every incoming student cohort. Universities are all too happy to trumpet research success stories while burying teaching and learning statistics in unpublished regulatory reports.

From every angle, Australia's regulation of teaching and learning seems designed to benefit universities, not their students. Sufficient data are available from the QILT surveys to construct a domestic performance index that ranks universities on the basis of metrics that are relevant to the core constituencies of public universities (i.e., students, parents, and governments), but there seems to be little interest in doing this. Undergraduate degrees could be structured in such a way as to facilitate the direct comparison of student outcomes across courses and universities, but the Commonwealth has chosen instead to empower universities to design their own degree courses—and to pay for whatever courses they offer. And instead of holding universities accountable for student success, the Job-ready Graduates Package holds students accountable, cutting off Commonwealth funding for students who fail 50% or more of their classes.

Certainly, there are students who fail because they don't take their classes seriously. But there are many more students who fail because they are unable to successfully navigate the transition from highly-structured K-12 schooling to relatively independent, self-monitored university work. Holding students (rather than universities) accountable for this is tantamount to punishing the victim. Chronically low levels of student engagement—the main takeaway finding from the QILT's student experience data—are symptomatic of arid learning environments, not student apathy. There is much that universities can do to engage students up-front, yet they generally wait until students are already failing, and even then intervene only with pro forma academic advising. If universities worked hard to make their classes and campuses exciting places to be, their students would engage right from the start, and be much less likely to fail out.

Another cause of failure is that universities allow students with very different levels of preparation to study alongside each other in the same classes via parallel admissions pathways. To continue the Sydney example, undergraduate psychology majors may have entered via degree courses with minimum adjusted ATARs ranging from 70 to 99.95. Even worse, among those with adjusted ATARs of 70, some have actual ATARs below 64. Students' ATAR adjustments may get them into the university, but they don't get them through. Indigenous applicants may have ATAR requirements waived entirely. Many other students are admitted without reference to their ATAR at all, if they have completed partial studies at other universities. Although data are not published that would make it possible to test the assertion, it seems mere common sense to surmise that many students with ATARs below 80 fail out of highly competitive programs like the University of Sydney's psychology major. The question is: why are they admitted in the first place?

Pernicious and potentially damaging market segmentation is not a practice limited to the University of Sydney. In fact, it is only possible to focus on Sydney's practices because the university is so much more forthcoming than most of its peers in providing the relevant data. The root problem has nothing to do with the University of Sydney or the field of psychology. It has to do with the structure of undergraduate degree courses in Australia and the incentives universities face to prioritise branding over educational outcomes. In this, the Commonwealth is fully complicit. Perhaps because government departments lack the independent expertise to question universities' motives, the Commonwealth has long acquiesced in the universities' self-serving insistence that institutional autonomy is the bedrock prerogative of university governance. In doing so, it has given short shrift to both students and taxpayers.

Of course, no government should seek to dictate what is taught in university classrooms. But governments have every right to dictate the terms on which teaching occurs. More than that: they have a responsibility, both to the students (to ensure the quality of teaching) and to the taxpayers (to ensure that their money is well-spent). The Australian government could generate strong pressures for improved undergraduate student outcomes by limiting universities to offering a modest number of well-defined, single-degree courses and then publishing uniform comparative data on student outcomes across universities for each degree. Currently, the Commonwealth legislates the macro-level structure within which Australian universities operate, but leaves the detailed design of the degree market to the universities. It should come as no surprise that the universities have structured that market to suit their own institutional priorities.

CHAPTER 7

Conclusion:
Can Australia's universities reform?

In 1952, the Australian Vice-Chancellors' Committee (AVCC) published a pamphlet to warn of 'A Crisis in the Finances and Development of the Australian Universities', with the words 'crisis' and 'Australian universities' highlighted on the title page.[141] Yet Australia's universities always had been in crisis (according to the AVCC) and always will be (according to its institutional successor, Universities Australia). Indeed, at the turn of the millennium the AVCC released another paper decrying twenty years of stagnant funding (1980-2000) and warning of the dire consequences of continued austerity.[142] It sparked a Senate inquiry on 'Universities in Crisis' that resulted in a recommendation that "the Government end the funding crisis in higher education by adopting designated Commonwealth programs involving significant expansion in public investment in the higher education system".[143] *Plus ça change.*

The coronavirus crisis, by comparison with past 'crises', really has compromised the finances of Australia's university system. But this crisis was largely self-made. A well-functioning university system would have ridden out the coronavirus pandemic like an island of stability in a sea of woe. Universities tend to have counter-cyclical revenue trends, as more young people choose study over employment when jobs are scarce and laid-off professionals take the opportunity to return to universities to pursue advanced degrees. Australia's current university financial crisis was caused by a perverse exploitation of international students for their revenue potential (far in excess of the pedagogical goal of increasing classroom diversity) compounded by poorly managed investments that paid off far worse than stock index funds or government bonds. By contrast, the top two sources of coronavirus-linked revenue declines at US universities were reduced parking fees and cafeteria sales.[144]

No Australian vice chancellor resigned to take responsibility for financial mismanagement in the wake of the coronavirus crisis. Instead, the vice chancellors trouped to Canberra—to demand a bailout. Their bailout narrative focused overwhelmingly on the need to preserve research capacity, despite the fact that dedicated research funding remained stable throughout the crisis. In Australia's university funding model, teaching supports the ordinary 'scholarship' of the teachers (i.e., the time academics devote to knowledge production), while the Commonwealth pays for "the systemic costs of research ... such as libraries, laboratories, consumables, computing centres and the salaries of support and technical staff" through its RSP block grants.[145] Block grants were first introduced in recognition of the fact that scientific research requires special facilities, in contrast to humanities scholarship, which generally only requires time for contemplation and writing.[146] These basic streams of Commonwealth support for university research were never threatened by the coronavirus crisis.

Of course, many Australian universities were using international student fee revenue to boost levels of big-ticket scientific research. But the modest decline in international student fee revenue experienced in 2020 should never have threatened Australian universities' financial stability, and would not have, had not so many universities grossly mismanaged their finances before the crisis. First, international student numbers should have been limited to levels that were appropriate for enriching the classroom environment, not been expanded to one-third of system-wide EFTSL. Second, international student fees should have been treated as a risky, volatile source of revenue, not built into universities' core financial models. Third, and most importantly, universities should have dedicated international student fee revenue primarily to the education of international students, not to unrelated strategic research initiatives. Had these basic managerial controls been in place, Australian universities would hardly have noticed the coronavirus disruption of international student enrolments.

In any case, the Commonwealth's $1 billion RSP top-up should have more than made up for any research shortfall. Yet Australia's universities continue to cry poor. That should come as no surprise: Australia's universities have always cried poor, even as they rose up the international rankings, provided comfortable salaries for their full-time employees, and dramatically expanded executive pay packages. Bowen's Law is in operation here, with the only limit on universities' spending (and consequently their ambitions) being the taxpayers' generosity. Even international student fee revenue hasn't offered a real alternative to taxpayer largesse, because Australian universities have systematically underpriced international student tuition. Had Australian universities priced international tuition in line with the total amounts paid on behalf of domestic students, they would likely have had far fewer international students to lose during the crisis.

Only the government's failure to properly monitor university finances has allowed universities to redirect international student fee revenue into strategic research initiatives. As anyone can see from browsing university media websites or reading Go8 press releases, these initiatives are the pride and glory of Australian universities (and their vice chancellors). Non-academics simply do not understand the extent to which research is the currency of academic prestige at both the individual and institutional levels. Most academics and universities teach students because they have to, not because they want to. Professorial recruiting is based almost entirely on research (and research funding) success, with teaching coming into play only as an afterthought. University rankings similarly focus overwhelmingly on research.

Universities seem almost to have convinced Australia's governments that they exist only to generate new knowledge, anchor development precincts, and generate export revenues. We often hear about universities' accomplishments in all of these areas. We rarely hear about universities' success in teaching Australian students. Teaching is treated as a simple numbers game: as long as enough Australian students are awarded university degrees—of whatever quality—everything is fine. Universities pursue research excellence, but teaching sufficiency. "The P gets the degree" applies to pass-level teaching just as much as to pass-level students. This mindset could be changed, but it only will be changed through government pressure. Left to themselves, universities, their vice chancellors, their trade associations, and their professors will never put the public interest ahead of their own.

A cap on international students

It is difficult to exaggerate the unwholesome extent to which Australian universities have overenrolled international students. No other major country's university system comes close to Australia's in its international student concentrations. Even in the European Union, where students can cross borders at will to study on the same terms as domestic students anywhere in the bloc, international student numbers are far below Australia's. Post-Brexit, some British universities are copying the Australian model, now that they are free to enroll unlimited numbers of non-EU students. Perhaps not surprisingly, they are doing it by leveraging Australian expertise, with several British universities having poached senior executives from Australia. The narrative that the UK is now out-competing Australia for Chinese students completely misses the fact that British universities have only recently opened the floodgates.[147] Australia's floodgates have been open for two decades.

Not for nothing have international students been called the 'cash cows' of the Australian university system.[148] They generated $10 billion in direct tuition revenue for Australian universities in 2019, plus an unknown amount in ancillary revenue from preparatory programs, housing rentals, and other services. Yet many international students struggle to succeed in "dysfunctional learning environments" where they often have few opportunities to meet local students or even practice their English.[149] Chinese students in particular routinely complain about a lack of English-language immersion, with some classes in economics and business so dominated by Chinese students that the primary language of group work is Chinese.[150] At the universities of Melbourne, Queensland, and Sydney, more than 80% of master-level business students hail from outside Australia. They are, in effect, studying in Australia to make business connections in China.

The 'cash cows' narrative was brought home to many people when the coronavirus crisis hit, stranding many international students in Australia without any means of support.[151] A spate of sympathetic news reports highlighted the travails of students who were struggling to make ends meet without access to JobSeeker and other government benefits.[152] Yet in principle it was perfectly reasonable for the Australian prime minister to tell international students that if "they're not in a position to be able to support themselves, then there is the alternative for them to return to their home countries", advising them to "make your way home ... to ensure that you can receive the supports that are available ... in your home countries".[153] It was perfectly reasonable, that is, under the official narrative that international students come to Australia to study, and must demonstrate adequate financial means to support themselves in Australia before receiving a visa.

In reality, everyone (except perhaps the government and the universities) knew that many international students pay for their courses out of the proceeds of their work in-country, often working excessive hours under exploitative conditions, in violation of their visa terms.[154] This situation is especially common among South Asian students, and is reflected in the steep fall-off in South Asian student numbers when teaching moved online. With prospective students unable to rely on employment income in Australia to support their studies, new commencements of Indian students at Australian higher education providers fell 65% between 2019 and 2021; for Nepali students, the decline was 37%; for Pakistanis, 45%; for Sri Lankans, 54%.[155] These countries are simply too poor to send large cohorts of international students to Australian universities based on family resources alone. For many South Asian students, a student visa is a very expensive but thinly disguised work visa.

The China rort differs from the India rort: instead of work permits, the universities are selling immigration places. Chinese student commencements fell only 25% in 2020, and actually bounced back in 2021—despite the borders being closed. The concentration of Chinese students in accounting programs (where they focus on learning Australian accounting standards) betrays their prime motivation for studying in Australia: an accounting certification is worth an extra ten points under the skilled migration program. The official line that relatively few students transition to permanent residence is based on analyses so flawed as to be almost useless: it considers only direct transitions from student to residence visas, while the skilled visa program points system strongly incentivises graduates to return home and apply for a residence visa 3-8 years later.[156] There are many routes from study to residence, and the percentage of former students who ultimately achieve permanent residence is much higher than government reports suggest.[157]

Only the government has access to the data that would allow a comprehensive calculation of the proportion of international students who transition to permanent residence, and the government has so far shown no interest in publishing this politically-sensitive information. But those figures shouldn't be politically sensitive, and wouldn't be, if universities were more responsible in their recruitment of international students. Australia is very welcoming to immigrants, and there's nothing wrong with students wanting to work in Australia or move to Australia after completing their degrees. Sensitivities only arise with the perception that universities are 'selling' the right to live and work in Australia. Had universities limited their recruitment of international students to levels that were consistent with their educational missions, international student numbers would be non-controversial. But many (in fact, most) Australian universities benchmark their international student recruitment targets to levels that are wildly inconsistent with pedagogical objectives. This must end.

A floor on international student fees

Australia's public universities have demonstrated that they can't be trusted with the autonomy to manage their own international student intake levels: the incentive structures facing universities are too far out of alignment with those of students and taxpayers for universities to be expected to act in the public interest. If international students really did generate higher per-EFTSL revenues than domestic ones, at least the public interest might not be harmed by universities' extraordinarily high international enrolments—though it is hard to see how the public would benefit. But given that international students are effectively free riding on the campus infrastructure provided by the Australian government for the benefit of Australian students, the continued recruitment of extraordinary numbers of international students is a scandal, pure and simple.

The Commonwealth should place pedagogically-appropriate limits on the number of international students Australian public universities are allowed to enroll. The exact proportions might be determined by an expert committee, but best practice comparisons suggest something along the lines of a maximum 20% international students in any particular degree course, 15% for each university overall, and 10% from any one country. Private universities might be allowed to offer courses primarily for the purpose of serving international students, but universities that receive public funds should not be competing in this space. To the extent that international students enrich the educational environment for domestic students, they should be welcomed. But it should be a condition of Commonwealth funding that publicly-supported universities operate primarily in the public interest.

As a corollary to international student caps, Commonwealth-supported universities should be required to set fees for international students at levels that are no lower than the per-student average amounts being paid on behalf of domestic students in the same courses. Much has been made of the stylised fact that international student tuition fees are generally three times the domestic student fees for the same courses. Even adding Commonwealth contributions to domestic student fees results in per-student revenues that are much lower than the fees paid by international students. But this comparison ignores the broad-spectrum support that Australian governments provide on behalf of domestic students. Absent the long-term infrastructural investments that Australian governments have made for sole purpose of educating domestic students, international students wouldn't even have campuses on which to study.

Australian Commonwealth structural support for university education includes concessional financing for Higher Education Loan Program loans, roughly $1 billion a year for medical research, another $1 billion for the ARC, roughly $2 billion for research block grants ($3 billion in 2021), and assorted special purpose grants for infrastructure. On top of this, the states have endowed universities with land and facilities. None of this is budgeted with reference to supporting individual students, but all of this is done for the ultimate purpose of educating the domestic student body as a whole. Institutions that do not educate domestic students are generally ineligible for any of these forms of support.

The need for higher international student fees may sound counter-intuitive, but the simple fact is that most international students in Australia are not paying the full costs of their education. To see this, imagine what might happen if an Australian public university were to split into separate domestic and international divisions. Under existing legislation, professors in both divisions would be eligible to compete for

Commonwealth research grants, benefit from Commonwealth research block grant support, work on state-provided campuses, use the library, and lie on the lawn. The domestic division would be supported by domestic student fees. The international division, charging much higher per-student fees, could use a portion of its student fee revenue to provide an equivalent educational experience for international students, and divert the rest to discretionary funds. On paper, this would look like a huge 'profit' from international education. In reality, it would represent little more than laundering government infrastructure funding into free cash flow.

This is what Australian public universities are doing right now with international student fee revenue. Were international student fees raised to levels that reflected the full costs of educating international students, far fewer international students would choose to study in Australia. The very fact that, pre-coronavirus, Australian universities showed themselves able to recruit essentially unlimited numbers of international students suggests that their product was underpriced. Raising international student tuition fees to the level of average per-student costs might in itself be enough to reduce international student numbers to pedagogically appropriate levels. It would, at least, be a step in the right direction. Fee floors should be used in conjunction with enrolment caps to enforce ethical university behaviour. Without them, universities will continue to game the system—and fleece the Australian taxpayer.

Clarity in research funding

Australia's endless squabbles over university funding, the international student blow-out, vice chancellors' rankings obsessions, and the emerging threat posed by foreign influence on campus all arise from a single, unlikely source: a lack of clarity about research. No one seems to know for sure what research is, who should do it, who should pay for it, or why they should pay for it. Government documents are inconsistent in their terminology and government ministers exhibit a complete historical amnesia in the formulation of research policy. Universities and their trade associations actually encourage this confusion, since it provides cover for their Commonwealth funding offensives and a smokescreen for their own unethical practices. Most higher education consultants and commentators are not themselves academics, and thus have little understanding of how research actually works. The whole system of research support at Australian universities is one giant—to use the polite word—mess.

The Australian government officially defines "research and experimental development" as "creative and systematic work undertaken in order to increase the stock of knowledge—including knowledge of humankind, culture and society—and to devise new applications of available knowledge".[158] This wording is derived directly from the OECD's 'Frascati Manual' guidelines for standardising the reporting of research and development activities across countries. The bit in the middle is an obvious fudge: after all, why wouldn't research include knowledge of humankind? The OECD didn't feel it necessary to mention that research includes knowledge of, say, gravity, or electrical engineering. The underlying reality is that until 2002 the Frascati Manual went under the title *Measurement of Scientific and Technical Activities*, which makes its origins clear enough. The original Frascati Manual, agreed at a conference in the Roman suburb of Frascati in 1963, defined research frankly as "work undertaken primarily for the advancement of scientific knowledge.[159]

A definition of research that excludes the humanities, the social sciences, the arts, and most of the professions would exclude more than half of all university academics, so the insertion of "humankind" into the Frascati formula was necessary. Nonetheless, the OECD continues to maintain that humanities scholarship can only be classified as 'research' if the "requirements for identifying the 'scientific' nature of such research are met".[160] And although "knowledge of humankind, culture and society" is now included in the definition of research, the technical criteria by which research is judged have never been updated to account for the kinds of research that are actually undertaken in the humanities and social sciences. Thus the Australian government follows the OECD in specifying that "for an activity to be an R&D activity it must satisfy <u>all five</u> core criteria:

(1) be aimed at new findings (novel)
(2) be based on original, not obvious, concepts and hypotheses (creative)
(3) be uncertain about the final outcomes (uncertain)
(4) be planned and budgeted (systematic)
(5) lead to results that could be possibly reproduced (transferable and/or reproducible)."[161]

Note especially point (4). The Frascati Manual expands on this requirement: "the purpose of the R&D project and the sources of funding for the R&D performed should be identified" in order for it to be classified as 'research'.[162] But what if a research project is not explicitly funded? A mathematician might prove a theorem in the bathtub. More controversially, scholars across the humanities, social sciences, business, and law routinely write books for which the only resource they need is their own time. If that time is not explicitly planned and budgeted, do their books not count as 'research'?

Under the *Higher Education Standards Framework (Threshold Standards) 2021*, Australian universities are required to engage in "research that leads to new knowledge". In order to demonstrate that they are meeting this requirement, universities must submit evidence to TEQSA that their research outputs (academic papers, books, and the like) meet certain benchmarks for breadth and quality. Yet in calculating universities' research expenditures, the DESE only recognises money that is derived from research grants, not time spent on writing books and papers. The strange result is that many of the 'research outputs' recognised by TEQSA as satisfying university's statutory research activity requirements are, technically speaking, unfunded, and thus by the government's own definitions they cannot constitute 'research'. Much of what TEQSA certifies as research is explicitly excluded from the DESE's research accounting.

This is ridiculous. Most permanent academic staff at Australian universities are classified as teaching and research academics, with an allocation of work time to teaching, research, and service on a 40-40-20 basis. Some are not so lucky, and have reduced research allocations, while a few are very lucky, and have increased research allocations. There is a trend toward the disaggregation of teaching and research, but the dominant form of academic employment in Australia remains 40-40-20.[163] With a wave of the bureaucratic wand, the Commonwealth could formally classify the pro-rated research share of academic salaries as research expenditures. To satisfy point (4) of the OECD's extended definition of research, this would merely require that every academic with a research loading produce a research plan for the year—something that every university should require anyway, and most already do. With this simple accounting reform, academic time spent on research activities would be properly credited, and non-science academics would suddenly be transformed into genuine 'researchers'.

As things stand, research that lacks grant funding is not officially counted as 'research' at all. Yet all 40-40-20 teaching-research-service academics are required to conduct research, and most of it is rated as being at or above 'world standard' by the ARC. This contradiction feeds into the universities' 'underfunding' narrative, but it is blatantly ahistorical. Systematic Commonwealth funding for university research began in 1936, when "a 5-year program was inaugurated by which £A30,000 was to be spent annually for grants to support research in the physical and biological sciences".[164] Early Commonwealth inquiries into university funding routinely cited the "special problems" posed by "the high cost of scientific and technological education and research".[165] As with OECD data definitions, the early emphasis of Commonwealth funding was on big science. It was taken for granted that non-scientific research could be funded out of ordinary tuition revenues, but that science research required extra funding.

Explicitly recording 40% of the salaries of ordinary 40-40-20 teaching-and-research academics as a form of research expenditure would bring university accounting into line with reality. It would also clarify the costs of educating international students. International student tuition fees should cover both the teaching and research allocations of their teachers' salaries, just as funding for Commonwealth-supported places supports the full salaries of 40-40-20 academics. After all, if the Commonwealth isn't paying for the 40% of professors' time that is nominally dedicated to research, who is? The universities might like us to believe that the answer is "international students", but the 40-40-20 allocation of professors' time was in place long before the recent run-up in international student numbers, and real Commonwealth funding per domestic student has been stable over time. If international students now pay for ordinary professors' research allocations, who paid for them twenty years ago?

In conjunction with this simple accounting reform, the Commonwealth should end the ARC's practice of offering research fellowships and associated research 'buy-outs' of teaching time. Ordinary academics already have time for research, and it is a waste of precious research dollars to use them to take top academics out of the classroom, "denying undergraduates the opportunity to be taught by academics at the height of their powers".[166] The roughly $200 million a year that the ARC spends on fellowships would be much better spent on the direct costs of the equipment that teaching-and-research academics need to conduct their research. Instead of giving an English professor several hundred thousand dollars to be freed from teaching for a few years, the ARC should be paying for research-critical facilities for a biologist or engineer.

There are legitimate costs for humanities and social science research, but time off teaching is not one of them. Nor is time off teaching for scientists. The whole point of locating research in universities is for students to be taught by academics who are research active. Indeed, the legislative requirement that universities engage in research at all was historically student-focused. Until the 1988 higher education funding reforms, the distinction between universities and colleges of advanced education was that university academics conducted research, while college teachers only needed to keep current with research developments—i.e., to engage in 'scholarship' about existing knowledge but not to conduct 'research' to create new knowledge.

The abolition of the distinction between colleges and universities was accomplished through the sleight-of-hand requirement that to qualify as a university, an institution had to show that it was producing research in at least a small number of fields. This transitional arrangement solidified into the pro forma fiction that 'research' is conducted by universities, not by individual academics. Unfortunately, that fiction has generated a series of perverse incentives for academics, universities, and governments to promote policies that are contrary to the best interests of Australian domestic students. It has led to a situation in which the most accomplished academics are encouraged to seek fellowships that liberate them from teaching to pursue research full-time, since by definition any activity that receives ARC funding is counted as research, and universities only have to demonstrate that someone employed by them is doing research, even if those people don't actually teach students. This is absolutely dysfunctional.

Worst of all, Australian governments (state and Commonwealth) seem to have bought into the separation of teaching and research. They seem to have forgotten why they started funding university research in the first place. Universities have encouraged this historical amnesia, which will inevitably come back to bite them. After all, why should Australian governments fund research into topics like gender representation in Renaissance painting, political opinion-formation in Uruguay, or the origins of the universe? These are hardly practical national priorities. Moreover, were the Commonwealth to strangely decide to commission such research, why should it commission such research from universities? Unless individual classroom teachers are expected to be research active, there is no obvious government interest in funding university research at all. Academics beware.

A fixed degree menu

Of course, research is expensive, and ensuring that all individual academics are reserved time for research makes it even more so. With the government always keen to expand access to university education, it can sometimes seem like the opportunity for every teacher to engage in research is a luxury that the country cannot not afford. If that is really the case, then the government should simply reestablish the colleges of advanced education. There is no logical case to be made that, within the same university and the same degree program, some students should be taught by full-time teachers while others are taught by teachers who also do research. If teaching by full-time teachers is of the same or higher quality as teaching by teacher-researchers, then all teaching should be done by full-time teachers and universities should give up on research. That would save the taxpayer quite a bit.

When the education minister mentioned the possibility of university specialisation in a June 2021 speech, higher education commentators immediately took it as an invitation to lobby for greater differentiation between research-and teaching-intensive universities.[167] It's not at all clear that that's what the minister meant by opening a conversation on "greater differentiation and specialisation in the university sector", but it was what (certain) universities wanted to hear.[168] Differentiation and specialisation might simply mean that some universities host law schools while others host medical schools, instead of a separation by research intensity (and thus, inevitably, prestige). After all, the minister continued by pointing out that Australia has "39 comprehensive universities, which may not be an optimal model for the quality of teaching or research in this country". It takes a sharp and perhaps self-interested eye to see in that an argument for teaching-intensive institutions.

Only a truly courageous politician would dare to designate particular (presumably rural and regional) universities as research-light, concentrating Commonwealth funding on (presumably) metropolitan, (presumably) Go8 universities. It would also go against the trend of the current government's push to increase research capacity in the regions.[169] The only politically realistic way to de-prioritise research in a way that does not exacerbate educational inequalities would be to designate certain disciplines as teaching-intensive. In other words, the government really would have to reestablish the colleges of advanced education. Assuming that the Commonwealth does not intend to re-relegate paraprofessional disciplines like teaching, nursing, allied health, pharmacy, music, art, design, accounting, journalism, paralegal studies, and criminal justice to non-university status, it must look for savings elsewhere.

The bipartisan 'efficiency dividend' of the mid-2010s was a more reasonable approach to cost-cutting (and the opportunity-expansion that it enables). But although successive governments demanded cost savings from universities, they failed to provide mechanisms through which those savings could be realised. As a result, universities responded by stonewalling while waiting for better days—and it didn't take long for the government to give in. No other outcome was ever really possible. The simple fact is that universities don't really know how to promote efficiencies. Their response to budget cuts is to petulantly reduce the quality of the education they offer by increasing class sizes, cutting back on student services, and having more classes taught by casual academics. In other words, they respond to political pressure by raising the political heat.

If the government wants to realise an efficiency dividend, it has to put in place a higher education market microstructure that rewards efficiency. A market microstructure defines the rules by which a market operates. For example, on the Australian Stock Exchange, stock options generally represent contracts for 100 shares, for delivery on the third Thursday of the month, at a series of predefined strike prices. This microstructure leaves only the value of the options contracts to be determined by market forces and ensures that options are valued transparently and efficiently. Contrast this with the market microstructure for mobile phone data plans. The Australian Competition & Consumer Commission allows mobile data providers wide latitude in setting contract terms, with the result that consumers are generally unable to directly compare the plans offered by different providers. Consumers are offered a variety of contract terms, but price discovery in the market as a whole is opaque and inefficient. It is very difficult for consumers to determine which providers offer the best plans.

Efficiency and transparency are not the only goals of market microstructure, and sometimes other priorities rightly predominate. Many might argue that universities should be free to innovate by offering bespoke degree courses tailored to meet individual student needs. Yet although the highest-performing American universities are extraordinarily free to innovate, they have arrived—subject to many minor fiddles—at a standard four year undergraduate degree course. The key difference between the American and Australian university markets isn't the microstructure; it's the macrostructure. In the United States, most students pay for their courses, either directly or via hard loans with fixed interest rates. In Australia, most of the costs are picked up by the government, and the residual student tuition payments are financed via a tax disguised as an interest-free loan. The American higher education market macrostructure disciplines universities to serve students. The Australian one encourages universities to serve themselves.

In essence, university degree courses in Australia aren't bought by students. They're bought by the government, which then turns around and offers them to students on a concessional basis. Under these conditions, students cannot realistically be expected to subject universities to market discipline. Notwithstanding the market-friendly rhetoric of the Job-ready Graduates Package, the price signals provided to students are so distorted by Commonwealth contributions, HELP loans, and broad government infrastructural support for university research and facilities as to be almost meaningless. In any case, Australian universities do not compete on price for domestic students. In theory, they compete on quality, but like mobile data providers, they have evolved a market microstructure so arcane that it makes direct quality comparisons between universities (or even between courses at the same university) next to impossible.

The Commonwealth, as the effective paying customer for most domestic undergraduate courses, should step in to reform the market microstructure for Australian university degrees. Assuming that the government will maintain its established practice of setting fixed prices for university courses, it should use its purchasing power to shape a standardised menu of degree courses that are eligible for Commonwealth support. Much as the Australian Stock Exchange sets the terms for options contracts, the Commonwealth should set the terms for university courses. But in the absence of price competition between universities, the government should use market forces to drive up the quality of the education universities provide at any (government-fixed) price.

To do this, the government should establish a fixed degree menu for Commonwealth supported places. To reduce costs and expand educational opportunities, the menu should be structured on the principles of one degree per course and one course per student. There is little rationale for the Commonwealth to fund multiple combined bachelor degrees in a single course, as it does now, instead of encouraging students to move on from their first bachelor degrees to master-level study. Taking the Melbourne Model as a guide, a limited number of no more than a dozen bachelor degrees should be approved for Commonwealth support, subject to revision on a five or (better) ten year cycle. And to help students compare the quality of degrees across universities, the DESE should make its QILT survey results available in a more accessible format, publishing degree-level scores alongside other relevant metrics like minimum ATARs, offer acceptance rates, average class sizes, and percent international students.

The standardisation of Commonwealth supported places on a one degree per course / one course per student basis would immediately free up tens of thousands of new university places (only the DESE has the data needed to determine exactly how many) at no extra cost to the taxpayer. Over time, it would also give the government the data it needs to increase efficiency and drive down costs. For example, the government could shift Commonwealth supported places from high-cost providers to low-cost providers by creating an auction-style market for degrees. Since the basic parameters of degree courses would be fixed across universities, the government could offer more places in any particular degree course to those universities that were willing to teach the course at a lower price point. Through this mechanism, the Commonwealth could use its purchasing power to drive "greater differentiation and specialisation in the university sector" by gradually shifting student load in particular subjects to the universities that prove themselves most able to teach them efficiently.

* * *

Can Australia's universities reform? They can, but they won't do it themselves. They must be reformed. The Commonwealth shouldn't meddle in the academic details of teaching and research, but it should actively intervene to ensure that Australia's public universities consistently act in the public interest. That means putting in place mechanisms to ensure that the interests of students and taxpayers are prioritised over those of professors and university administrators. Universities should be reminded, in no uncertain terms, that although they are autonomous, they are not independent. Australia's university system stands in dire need of institutional reform, and as the primary regulator and funder of the country's university system, the Australian government must take the lead in forcing it through.

Too often, and for too long, Australian governments have enabled university behaviours that broadly disserve Australia's students and effectively defraud Australia's taxpayers. Governments headed by both major parties have allowed (and even encouraged) universities to expand international student enrolments beyond all sound pedagogical limits. They have meanwhile picked up most of the tab for research and infrastructure, allowing universities to launder international student fee revenue into purely discretionary funds. They have applauded the universities' international rankings success, despite its being achieved at the cost of degraded educational experiences for domestic students. And despite an impressive display of political fireworks, the current government shows no signs of meaningfully intervening to curtail inappropriate Chinese influence on campus.

The Commonwealth funds the universities in trust for students, taxpayers, and all of society. In discharging this duty, it should act as a true trustee. Instead of enabling the self-interested behaviour of Australian universities, cutting a bit here and intervening a bit there, it should insist that universities deliver—first and foremost—a quality education for Australian domestic students. It should remember that it began to explicitly fund research 85 years ago in order to ensure that Australian universities could attract research-active scientists to teach its domestic students, and structure its research funding in line with that purpose. It should put in place mechanisms that help students evaluate the relative quality of each university's offerings, then use those mechanisms to promote a race to the top. It should seek to cut costs by consistently nudging students toward more efficient providers, not by making headline-grabbing demands for savings, then quietly abandoning them in favour of business as usual.

Universities prize their operational and intellectual autonomy, but with autonomy comes responsibility, and all the more so when that autonomy is purchased at the expense of the taxpayer. Over the last two decades, many of Australia's public universities have acted irresponsibly—in their bloated international student recruitment programs, in their unbridled pursuit of international rankings, in their don't ask, don't tell approach to Chinese influence, and in their outright exploitation of domestic students, who are in fact the real 'cash cows' of the Australian university system. Governments of all stripes have tolerated these irresponsible behaviours, perhaps out of a respectful confidence in the universities' competence and goodwill. More likely, long-term government complacency has been the result of a profound ignorance of how the university system really works.

Autonomy is a wonderful privilege, but everyone needs limits. Right now, the universities don't quite get a blank cheque, but they do get a generous allowance with very few strings attached. They evade responsibility by hiding their less salubrious behaviours from public scrutiny—with the full complicity of their regulators. Details about international students, research grants, vice chancellor compensation contracts, and China collaborations are all kept secret. As a case in point: every freedom of information request filed in the course of researching this book was denied. Data requests sent to TEQSA, the DESE, and the QILT program also went unanswered or unfulfilled. The foreign influence public registry created under the AFRA contains the names of university agreements, but none of the details. The proposals under which the ARC hands out millions of dollars of taxpayer money are treated as commercial-in-confidence documents. If many of the insights offered in this book are not backed up by detailed statistics, it is only because the universities and their regulators won't provide the requisite data. Stonewalling is their default response to all requests.

Academics consistently advocate transparency in governance—except when it comes to their own institutions. Universities, heal thyselves. It seems hard to believe that Australian universities would behave as they do if the full details of their actions were in the public domain. Why should it take an anonymous whistleblower and the exercise of parliamentary privilege for the public to discover the incentive terms of a vice chancellor's contract? What could be so embarrassing or improper about the objectives that a university sets for its vice chancellor that they have to be kept secret? The public will probably never know the answers to these, as to so many questions about Australia's public universities. That is flat-out disgraceful. Perhaps the most important first step in reforming Australian universities is simply to apply the time-honoured principle that sunlight is the best disinfectant. After all, even an ivory tower does not shine by its own light.

Endnotes

1 John Ross, 2021, 'Covid triggers change of guard in Australian sector leadership', *Times Higher Education*, March 17.

2 Gareth Evans and Brian Schmidt, 2018, 'Why ANU knocked back the Ramsay Centre course ', *The Australian*, June 26.

3 Michael Spence, 2019, 'Sorry, Ramsay Centre, but our academic freedom was never on the table: Sydney Uni chief responds', *Sydney Morning Herald*, December 6.

4 Tony Abbott, 2018, 'Paul Ramsay's vision for Australia', *Quadrant*, May 24.

5 Judith Brett, 2021, 'The bin fire of the humanities', *The Monthly* 175(March): 20-27.

6 Robert French, 2019, 'Report of the independent review of freedom of speech in Australian higher education providers, DESE, page 13.

7 Unsigned, undated, 'Glossary of terms in Part A of the Higher Education Standards Framework 2015', TEQSA, retrieved June 20, 2021.

8 Richard Ferguson, 2021, 'Elite universities submit 4000 foreign deals for Marise Payne to scrutinise and possibly cancel', *The Australian*, June 15.

9 Go8, undated, 'About the Go8', retrieved June 22, 2021.

10 Batchelor Institute of Indigenous Tertiary Education, 2014, 'Staff code of conduct, March 8, paragraph 7.5.

11 University of Sydney Act 1850 (NSW).

12 University of Melbourne Act 1853 (VIC).

13 James Guthrie, 2021, 'The charitable purpose of Macquarie University is to advance education', Campus Morning Mail, September 14.

14 Catriona Jackson, 2021, 'Universities Australia argues the sector's case for federal support', *The Australian*, June 1.

15 Unsigned, 2015, 'Australia's university system efficient but underfunded', Universities Australia, May 21.

16 Rebecca Galdies, 2020, 'Fund unis fairly', NTEU, August 7.

17 Labor Party shadow education minister, Tanya Plibersek, as quoted by Naaman Zhou, 2021, 'Australian universities brace for "ugly" 2022 after budget cuts', *The Guardian*, May 13.

18 Go8 CEO Vicki Thomson, as quoted by Richard Ferguson, 2020, 'Group of Eight warns of "brain drain" with 7000 jobs set to go', *The Australian*, July 17.

19 Go8 chair Peter Hoj, as quoted by Unsigned, 2017, 'Go8 Media Release: Go8 disheartened and dismayed by Government's treatment of Australia's young people', Go8, December 18.

20 ANU vice chancellor Brian Schmidt, as quoted by Conor Duffy, 2021, 'Universities are being "left to bleed" after 2021 federal budget snub, Nobel Laureate ANU head says', *ABC News*, May 14.

21 Jack Derwin, 2021, 'The government is slashing university funding to the lowest levels in decades, as the sector faces $3.8 billion in losses', *Business Insider*, April 27.

22 Richard Holden, 2020, 'Vital signs: This university funding crisis was always coming—COVID-19 just accelerated it', *The Conversation*, August 14.

23 James Guthrie, Martina Linnenluecke, Ann Martin-Sardesai, Yun Shen, and Tom Smith, 2021, 'On the resilience of Australian public universities: Why our institutions may fail unless vice-chancellors rethink broken commercial business models', *Accounting & Finance* preprint, page 29.

24 James Guthrie, 2021, 'How Deakin U perceives its purpose: It's in the annual reports', Campus Morning Mail, September 27.

[25] Madeleine Morris, 'Superannuation returns are flat—but don't panic just yet, says super boss', ABC News, June 18.

[26] Janet Lorin, 2021, 'U.S. college endowments post best annual performance since 1986 ', Bloomberg, August 3.

[27] John Ross, 2020, 'Australian PM: "No special deal" for universities on bailouts', *Times Higher Education*, July 21.

[28] Innovative Research Universities executive director Conor King, as quoted by Paul Karp, 2020, 'Australian universities angry at "final twist of the knife" excluding them from jobkeeper', *The Guardian*, May 4.

[29] Unsigned, 2021, *Education at a Glance 2020*, OECD, Table C1.2 (page 281).

[30] Jeannie Rea, 2018, 'More money in the system but less certainty', *The Australian*, November 13.

[31] Unsigned, 2019, *Higher Education: Facts and Figures*, Universities Australia, page 14.

[32] Vicki Thomson, 2016, 'The bipartisan university policy vacuum—cuts, neglect and underinvestment', *Australian Financial Review*, April 21.

[33] Geoff Sharrock, 2019, 'Australia's tertiary education spending grew while commentators cried otherwise: We explain in 6 charts', *The Conversation*, November 26.

[34] Unsigned, 2020, *Education at a Glance 2020*, OECD, Table C2.2 (page 293), column 7.

[35] Unsigned, 2020, *Education at a Glance 2020*, OECD, Table C1.2 (page 281), column 7.

[36] Unsigned, undated, World and Young University Rankings 2021, Times Higher Education.

[37] Deloitte Access Economics, 2019, *Transparency in Higher Education Expenditure*, DESE.

[38] John H. Howard, 2021, *Rethinking Australian Higher Education: Towards a Diversified System for the 21st Century*, Howard Partners, page 2.

39 Unsigned, 1998, 'Learning for life: Review of higher education financing and policy [West Report]', Department of Employment, Education, Training and Youth Affairs, April 17, page 64.

40 Tony Adams, 1998, 'The operation of transnational degree and diploma programs: The Australian case', *Journal of Studies in International Education* 2(1): 3-22.

41 Jenna Price, 2020, 'Why has the government waged war on our universities?', *Canberra Times*, May 15.

42 Jackson Gothe-Snape, 2018, 'Australian National University to halt student enrolment growth', ABC News, July 24.

43 Brian Schmidt, 2021, 'Universities have been left to bleed in the budget but we are pivotal to the recovery', *The Guardian*, May 12.

44 Salvatore Babones, 2019, 'The China student boom and the risks it poses to Australian universities', Centre for Independent Studies, Table 2 (page 22).

45 Salvatore Babones, 2019, 'The China student boom and the risks it poses to Australian universities', Centre for Independent Studies, Table 9 (page 28).

46 Sian Powell, 2018, 'Business schools grapple with number of Chinese students', *The Australian*, June 27.

47 Salvatore Babones, 2020, 'Is there a future for international Chinese students in Australia?', pp. 37-42 in *UK Universities and China* (edited by Michael Natzler), Higher Education Policy Institute, Table 1 (page 40).

48 Naaman Zhou, 2021, ' Universities discount fees for international students stuck outside Australia', *The Guardian*, February 1.

49 Unsigned, undated, 'Defence at a glance', Department of Defence, retrieved July 2, 2021.

50 Howard Bowen, as paraphrased by Andrew Norton, 2014, 'Higher education reform clarifier #5: Would arts degrees need to cost twice as much?', andrewnorton.net.au, June 1.

51 Howard R. Bowen, 1980, *The Costs of Education*, Jossey-Bass Publishers.

[52] Robert Martin and Andrew Gillen, 2009, 'Breaking the cost spiral', *Inside Higher Ed*, August 7.

[53] Unsigned, undated, 'Where do HE students come from?', Higher Education Statistics Agency, retrieved July 5, 2021.

[54] Unsigned, 2019, 'Rethink China: The end of the affair', Education Rethink.

[55] Salvatore Babones, 2020, 'Coronavirus crisis may spell the end of an era for international education', *Times Higher Education*, March 22.

[56] Unsigned, undated, 'About the Market Information Package', retrieved July 5, 2021.

[57] Unsigned, undated, 'Where do HE students come from?', Higher Education Statistics Agency, retrieved July 5, 2021.

[58] Salvatore Babones, 2019, 'The China student boom and the risks it poses to Australian universities', Centre for Independent Studies, page 17.

[59] Unsigned, 2021, 'Universities 2020 audits', Audit Office of New South Wales, June 18, page 23.

[60] Tim Dodd, Adam Creighton, and Jill Rowbotham, 2020, 'Top universities face $1.2bn coronavirus hit', *The Australian*, February 19.

[61] Frank Larkins and Ian Marshman, 2020, '$7.6 billion and 11% of researchers: Our estimate of how much Australian university research stands to lose by 2024', *The Conversation*, September 22.

[62] Geoff Chambers and Tim Dodd, 2020, 'Universities on the brink of "ground zero"', *The Australian*, June 2.

[63] Dan Tehan, 2020, 'Critical support for Australian university research', DESE, December 14.

[64] Unsigned, 2011, *Annual report 2010*, University of Melbourne, page 31.

[65] Andrew Norton, 2020, 'University research funding and international student numbers rose, and will likely fall, together', *EduResearch Matters*, July 6.

[66] Tim Dodd, 2021, 'UNSW's big spend on research reversed its

efficiency gains', *The Australian*, July 13.

67 Frank Larkins and Ian Marshman, 2020, '$7.6 billion and 11% of researchers: our estimate of how much Australian university research stands to lose by 2024', *The Conversation*, September 22.

68 Alan Tudge, 2021, 'Lifting the impact of universities to strengthen Australia's future', Office of Alan Tudge MP, February 26.

69 Gwilym Croucher, 2021, 'Australian universities may be at a turning point in the rankings chase. So what next?', *The Conversation*, March 18.

70 Nancai Liu (2015), 'The story of Academic Ranking of World Universities', *International Higher Education* 54: 2-3, page 2.

71 Unsigned, undated, 'About us', ShanghaiRanking Consultancy, retrieved July 9, 2021.

72 Robert Morse and Eric Brooks, 2020, 'How U.S. News calculated the 2021 best colleges rankings', *U.S. News & World Report*, September 13.

73 Yudhijit Bhattacharjee, 2011, 'Saudi universities offer cash in exchange for academic prestige', *Science* 334 (6061): 1344-1345.

74 Aparna Basu. 2006, 'Using ISI's "Highly Cited Researchers" to obtain a country level indicator of citation excellence', *Scientometrics* 68: 361-375; Luc Bauwens, Giordano Mion, and Jacques-François Thisse, 2011, 'The resistible decline of European science', *Recherches Économiques de Louvain* 77(4): 5-31.

75 Gwilym Croucher and James Waghorne, 2020, *Australian Universities: A History of Common Cause*, Sydney: UNSW Press, page 45.

76 Sean Emery, 2021, 'Big questions must be addressed to ensure research success', *The Australian*, June 30.

77 Brian J. Miller and Kyle Richardville, 2019, 'The NIH needs to become leaner and more innovative. Here's how to do that', *Stat*, January 22.

78 Heidi Ledford, 2014, 'Indirect costs: Keeping the lights on', *Nature*, November 19.

79   Unsigned, 2018, ' Guidance note: Scholarship, version 2.5', TEQSA, December 12.

80   Unsigned, 2020, 'Commonwealth scholarships guidelines (research) 2017, Federal Register of Legislation, July 23.

81   Unsigned, 2015, *Frascati Manual 2015*, Paris: OECD, page 44.

82   Unsigned, 2015, *Frascati Manual 2015*, Paris: OECD, page 45.

83   Unsigned, 2015, *Frascati Manual 2015*, Paris: OECD, page 57.

84   Unsigned, 2018, ' Guidance note: Research and research training, version 1.3', TEQSA, July 5.

85   Fergus Hunter, 2020, 'Liberal senator hits out at university China reliance, reveals whistleblower documents', *Sydney Morning Herald*, May 13.

86   James Paterson, 2020, *Senate Official Hansard*, May 12, page 2183.

87   Salvatore Babones, 2020, 'Update on Chinese student numbers at Australia's Go8 universities', personal website, February 11.

88   Salvatore Babones, 2019, *The China Student Boom and the Risks It Poses to Australian Universities*, Sydney: Centre for Independent Studies, page 12.

89   Jessica Chen Weiss, 2018, 'Cornell University suspended two exchange programs with China's Renmin University. Here's why', *The Washington Post*, November 1.

90   Unsigned, 2016, 'Strategic research spokes', Australian Centre on China in the World, October 6.

91   Unsigned, undated, 'China Studies Centre: Researching global issues in China', University of Sydney China Studies Centre, retrieved July 20, 2021.

92   Louise Templeton, 2018, 'UNSW officially opens its first overseas research centre in China', UNSW Newsroom, November 21.

93   James Laurenceson, 2017, 'Chinese students in Australia: A critical examination of recent media coverage', ACRI, November.

94   Unsigned, 2019, 'Guidelines to counter foreign interference in the Australian university sector', University Foreign Interference Taskforce, November.

95   Richard Ferguson, 2021, 'Elite universities submit 4000 foreign

deals for Marise Payne to scrutinise and possibly cancel', *The Australian*, June 15.

96 John Power, 2021, 'Confucius Institutes at Australian universities could be the next casualty of strained Beijing-Canberra ties', *South China Morning Post*, May 28.

97 Unsigned, 2019, 'Review of foreign government / organisation support for language education in NSW government schools', NSW Department of Education, page 5.

98 Sean Rubinsztein-Dunlop, 2019, 'The Chinese government co-funded at least four University of Queensland courses', ABC News, October 15.

99 Shannon Molloy, 2020, 'Australian university teaching pro-China class that amounts to propaganda, critics say', News.com.au, July 3.

100 Lisa Visentin, 2021, 'China-backed Confucius Institutes face closure under veto laws', *Sydney Morning Herald*, May 10.

101 Fergus Hunter, 2019, 'Universities must accept China's directives on Confucius Institutes, contracts reveal', *Sydney Morning Herald*, July 25; Fergus Hunter, 2019, 'RMIT granted Beijing authority over teaching at Confucius Institute', *Sydney Morning Herald*, October 1.

102 Thomas Lum, 2019, 'Confucius Institutes in the United States: Selected issues', Congressional Research Service, April 15.

103 Laura Walters, 2019, 'Chinese institute expands influence in Auckland', *Newsroom*, February 26.

104 Rebecca Zhu, 2021, 'It's "way past the time" for Confucius Institutes to close: Expert', *Epoch Times*, May 19.

105 James Laurenceson and Michael Zhou, 2019, 'Partners in knowledge creation: Trends in Australia-China research collaboration and future challenges', ACRI, July, page 1.

106 James Laurenceson and Michael Zhou, 2020, 'The Australia-China science boom', ACRI, July, Table 2 (page 9).

107 James Laurenceson and Michael Zhou, 2020, 'The Australia-China science boom', ACRI, July, Table 1 (page 8).

108 Michael Batty, 2003, 'The geography of scientific citation', *Environment and Planning A* 35: 761-770, Table 2 (page 763).

109 John Power, 2021, 'Chinese spying fears revived by security probe into Australian universities', *South China Morning Post*, February 11.

110 Su Zhou, 2017, 'Returnees finding big opportunities', *China Daily*, February 25.

111 Unsigned, 2020, 'Harvard University professor and two Chinese nationals charged in three separate China related cases', US Department of Justice, January 28.

112 Sharri Markson, 2020, 'How the CCP recruits our best and brightest', *The Australian*, August 24.

113 Sharri Markson and Kylar Loussikian, 2020, 'China exploits Australia's lax laws to sign up researchers for secretive program', *The Australian*, August 24.

114 Alex Joske, 2020, 'Hunting the phoenix: The Chinese Communist Party's global search for technology and talent', Australian Strategic Policy Institute, Research Report 35, page 3.

115 Olivia Caisley, 2020, 'Australian academics "in the dark" on Thousand Talents program', *The Australian*, September 4.

116 Unsigned, 2019, 'Guidelines to counter foreign interference in the Australian university sector', University Foreign Interference Taskforce, November.

117 Max Maddison, 2021, 'China has recruited "hundreds" of academics', *The Australian*, January 20.

118 Alex Joske, 2020, 'Hunting the phoenix: The Chinese Communist Party's global search for technology and talent', Australian Strategic Policy Institute, Research Report 35, page 28.

119 Louisa Bochner, 2020, 'China's influence on our campuses', Australian Strategic Policy Institute, August 31.

120 Unsigned, 2017, '2016 Student Experience Survey', DESE, March, page 51.

121 Unsigned, 2021, '2020 Student Experience Survey', DESE, March, page 4 (Table 1).

122 Unsigned, 2020, '2019 Student Experience Survey', DESE, March, pages 16-17 (Figure 4).

123 Unsigned, 2021, '2020 Employer Satisfaction Survey', DESE, March, page 3.

124 John Howard, 2021, *Rethinking Australian Higher Education: Towards a Diversified System for the 21st Century*, Howard Partners, page 289.

125 Emil Temnyalov, 2020, 'Some Australian universities might have to merge—and that's not necessarily a bad thing', *The Conversation*, August 24.

126 Unsigned, 2021, '17,000 uni jobs lost to COVID-19', Universities Australia, February 3.

127 Madeleine Heffernan, 2021, 'Casuals bore the brunt as COVID drove unis to shed 7500 jobs', *The Age*, May 12.

128 John Ross, 2021, 'New wave of redundancies sweeps Australian universities ', *Times Higher Education*, July 18.

129 Judith Brett, 2021, 'The bin fire of the humanities', *The Monthly* 175(March): 20-27, page 24.

130 Jordan Baker, 2021, 'The universities with the most unhappy students during the pandemic', *Sydney Morning Herald*, March 19.

131 Unsigned, 2021, '17,000 uni jobs lost to COVID-19', Universities Australia, February 3.

132 Chris Impey, 2020, 'Massive online open courses see exponential growth during COVID-19 pandemic', *The Conversation*, July 23; Dhawal Shah, 2020, 'The second year of the MOOC: A review of MOOC stats and trends in 2020', *The Report*, December 24.

133 Tony Wan, 2021, 'Coursera's IPO filing shows growing revenue and loss during a pandemic', EdSurge, March 5.

134 Unsigned, 2021, '2020 Student Experience Survey', DESE, March, page 44.

135 Natalie Skead, Fiona McGaughey, Kate Offer, Liam Elphick, and Murray Wesson, 2020, 'Lecture recordings mean fewer students are turning up—does it matter?', *The Conversation*, February 24.

136 Lillian Corbin, Kylie Burns, April Chrzanowski, 2010, 'If you

teach it, will they come? Law students, class attendance and student engagement', *Legal Education Review* 20(1): Article 3.

137 Unsigned, 2021, '2020 Employer Satisfaction Survey', DESE, March, pages 33-34.

138 TEQSA, undated, 'Glossary of terms in Part A of the Higher Education Standards Framework 2015', retrieved June 20, 2021.

139 Unsigned, 2021, 'Annual Report 2020', University of Western Australia, page 18.

140 Unsigned, 2021, 'Job-Ready Graduates Package', DESE, February 15.

141 Gwilym Croucher and James Waghorne, 2020, 'Universities in crisis? They've been there before, and found a way out', *The Conversation*, November 5.

142 Ian Chubb, 2000, 'Our universities: Our future: An AVCC discussion paper', AVCC, page 12.

143 Unsigned, 2001, 'Universities in crisis', Senate Standing Committees on Education and Employment, page 12.

144 Scott Friedman, Timothy Hurley, and Tiffany Fishman, 2020, 'COVID-19's impact on higher education: Strategies for tackling the financial challenges facing colleges and universities', Deloitte Center for Higher Education Excellence, page 1.

145 Unsigned, undated, 'Research support program', DESE, retrieved September 10, 2021.

146 Gwilym Croucher and James Waghorne, 2020, *Australian Universities: A History of Common Cause*, UNSW Press, pages 45-46.

147 Lisa Visentin and Eryk Bagshaw, 2020, 'Australia in race against UK, Canada, China to keep university students', *Sydney Morning Herald*, September 18.

148 Unsigned, 2019, 'Cash Cows', ABC News, May 6.

149 Robert Burton-Bradley, 2018, 'Poor English, few jobs: Are Australian universities using international students as 'cash cows'?', ABC News, November 25.

150 Sian Powell. 2018. 'Business schools grapple with number of

Chinese students', *The Australian*, June 27.

[151] Robert Bolton, 2020, 'Struggling international students don't get any JobSeekers', *Australian Financial Review*, April 13.

[152] Avneet Arora, 2020, '"We also need financial aid": International students seek government help as COVID-19 spreads', SBS Punjabi, March 17.

[153] Scott Morrison, 2020, 'Press Conference—Australian Parliament House', April 3.

[154] Caleb Goods, Alex Veen, and Tom Barratt, 2017, 'Being exploited and breaching your visa: The limited choices of the food delivery worker', *The Conversation*, August 21.

[155] Unsigned, 2021, 'International student data 2021', DESE, retrieved September 12.

[156] Hazel Ferguson and Harriet Spinks, 2021, 'Overseas students in Australian higher education: A quick guide', Australian Parliamentary Library, April 22.

[157] Andrew Norton, 2021, 'International students and permanent residence', May 31.

[158] Unsigned, 2021, 'Draft higher education research data collection specifications for the collection of 2021 data', DESE, September, page 5.

[159] Unsigned, 1963, Proposed Standard Practice for Surveys of Research and Development, OECD, page 12.

[160] Unsigned, 2015, *Frascati Manual 2015*, OECD, page 75.

[161] Unsigned, 2021, 'Draft higher education research data collection specifications for the collection of 2021 data', DESE, September, page 5.

[162] Unsigned, 2015, *Frascati Manual 2015*, OECD, page 47.

[163] Andrew Norton, 2020, 'Why did universities become reliant on international students? Part 4: Trying to maintain a teaching-research academic workforce', June 5.

[164] S. Encel, 1961, 'Financing scientific research in Australia', *Science* 134(3474): 260-266, page 262.

[165] Keith Murray, 1967, 'Report of the Committee on Australian

Universities', Commonwealth of Australia, page 68.

[166] Judith Brett, 2021, 'The bin fire of the humanities', *The Monthly* 175(March): 20-27, pages 23-24.

[167] Stephen Parker, Keith Houghton, and Mark Clisby, 2021, 'Why Alan Tudge is right to talk about specialisation in universities', *The Australian*, June 8.

[168] Alan Tudge, 2021, 'Our priorities for strengthening Australia's universities', DESE, June 3.

[169] Alan Tudge and Bridget McKenzie, 2021, '$20 million to boost research capacity at regional universities', DESE, September 7.